BASIC TRAINING FOR CHRISTIANS:
CHRISTIANS:
7 THINGS EVERY
CHRISTIAN
SHOULD KNOW

BASIC TRAINING FOR CHRISTIANS

7

THINGS EVERY CHRISTIAN SHOULD KNOW

DONNA ROWLETTE

XULON PRESS

Xulon Press
2301 Lucien Way #415
Maitland, FL 32751
407.339.4217
www.xulonpress.com

Unless otherwise indicated, scripture quotations are taken
from The New International Version (NIV). Copyright
© 1973, 1978, 1984, 2011 by Biblica, Inc.™. Used by
permission. All rights reserved.

Printed in the United States of America.

ISBN-13: 978-1-54565-871-0

Table of Contents

Introduction

In early 1984, I was preparing to graduate from high school and was unsure of what to do with myself next. I did not think I was smart enough for college, and I was searching for purpose. I was on the bus on my way home when I saw an army poster in front of a recruitment station that stated, "Be All You Can Be." I jumped off the bus, and before I knew it, I had joined the United States Army Reserves. A few months after graduating from high school, I received my first set of military orders which declared:

You are ordered to Initial Active Duty for Training (IADT) under Section 511 (d), Title 10, United States Code. Upon completion

of the training period shown below, unless sooner relieved or extended by proper authority, you will return to your parent unit. Proceed from your current home address, shown above, and report to this station not later than 0700 on 27 December 1984 and then:

Report to: US Army Reception Station FORT JACKSON, SC

Reporting Date: 28 DECEMBER 1984

Advanced Individual Training (AIT) location: SAME AS ABOVE

AIT Reporting Date: 22 February 1985

Training period: Approximately 19 weeks or completion of basic and Military Occupational Specialty (MOS) training

Immediately upon reading the order the spirit of fear rushed in like a storm. *Oh no!* I thought. *What have I gotten myself into?* I had just recently graduated from high school, and now I have to go to basic training two days after Christmas. *Christians don't go to basic training two days after Jesus's birthday*, I reasoned. Plus, it was too cold to be in basic training in December! After a few phone calls and pleas, I could calm my fears a little when I learned that my start date could be rescheduled. I was still a civilian at this time and had yet to embrace the army way. God hadn't given me the spirit of fear, but the spirit of fear was truly present. Originally, I was going in on the buddy system, but my buddy had backed out months earlier. Now, I was contemplating backing out too.

Within weeks, I received an amended set of orders with a new report date, April 1, 1985. *Is this an April fool's joke*, I thought? But it was not a joke. On April 1, 1985, I found myself at Fort Jackson, South Carolina, reporting to the US Army Reception Station. Unlike the name implied, there was not a pleasant welcome. I flew from Maryland to the local airport in South Carolina and was bused to the base. Upon arrival, the transformation process began. Like the book of Genesis in the Bible, there were a lot of first-time experiences I was about to embark on. I had my first airplane ride, my first time away from home, and my first interaction with various cultures. It was also my first time sharing a living space with so many ladies, which required me to strategize how to successfully start my day, but my biggest first would be my first experience with a drill sergeant. This experience would lead me to fully embrace Philippians 4:13 (KJV), "I can do all things through Christ which strengtheneth me."

Over the next eight weeks, Philippians 4:13 would become my lifeline. Those ten little words would carry me through road marches, would be with me while I slept in the fox hole I had dug myself, would comfort me while I low crawled on my back under barb wire, and when my drill sergeant was standing over me yelling at the top of his voice telling me that I wasn't army material. I would just silently recite the apostle Paul's words: "I can do all things through Christ which strengtheneth me," over and over again. Many times, during basic training I questioned why I volunteered for what seemed to be extremely unnecessary abuse of power. But basic training, as well as many other military training courses I would experience during my twenty years of service, proved helpful to mold and shape me into the person I am today.

The purpose of basic training was a big one. The United States Army was determined to transform me from a civilian with a "me mentality" to a soldier with a "team focus." This transformation process was not going to be easy. From the moment I arrived at the training center, I discerned that life as I once knew it would never be the same. The days were long; the training was hard, and the yelling was often. I learned a new way to tell time and the language was not quite the same. Even the way I leisurely enjoyed a meal was, for now, a thing of the past. Army leadership was determined to change my thought process and create in me a disciplined, self-confident, respectful, selfless soldier who would be loyal to her country, who would serve with honor, integrity, and courage (Fort Jackson Public Affairs Office 2016), even if it meant I had to lay down my life. As the cadence goes, "They took away my favorite jeans, and now I'm wearing army greens." I wore what they told me to wear, spoke how they instructed me to speak, and learned what they wanted me to learn. All as a part of the transformation process.

No longer was I concerned with being the original God destined me to be. For the next nineteen weeks, I was the property of the United States Army, and I was quickly informed that I was responsible for taking care of army property, yes me! I ate quickly what was given to me; I exercised as I was trained; I learned the army doctrine to become a better me and conformed to everything the army wanted me to do, no questions asked. I was told to shut up, listen, obey, learn quickly, and answer respectfully only when asked. The transformation process saturated every area of my life. The way I made my bed in the past—wrong! The way I folded my clothes in the past—wrong! The way I wore my hair—wrong! Even the alphabet I had learned from age two or three changed.

Although I could have done without the gas chamber experience, basic training proved to be a life-defining period. The pride I experienced after graduating from basic training, and later AIT, was something I had never experienced before. If you were a soldier, you were set apart. You were chosen, trained, molded, and shaped for service to your country. You were a part of a large family with members in every state in the United States. Basic training was just the beginning of your training in the military. Throughout your career, there would be many training requirements to help you successfully progress and to allow you to "Be All You Can Be." Basic training is not enough to equip you for your entire journey, but it is the start of creating your firm foundation.

Every Christian would benefit from developing a firm foundation to start their Christian journey. We need to learn a new language by studying the Word of God. We need to be able to articulate basic information about our Christian faith. As Christians, we should be so sure of God's love for us, that we never stop serving Him. We need to know that we are members of a Christian family that extends to every continent in the world, and we need to share the message to help grow our Christian family.

This basic training guide is not enough to equip you for your entire journey, but it is a start for creating your firm foundation. Romans 12:1-2 states:

"Therefore, I urge you, brothers and sisters, in view of God's mercy, to offer your bodies as a living sacrifice, holy and pleasing to God— this is your true and proper worship. Do not conform to the pattern of this world, but be transformed by the renewing of your mind. Then you will be able to test and approve what God's will is—His good, pleasing and perfect will."

In the next few chapters of this book, I will discuss why: renewing your mind must be intentional, embracing the theologian inside you is rewarding, recognizing the power of prayer is uplifting, knowing the Holy Spirit is your keeper is energizing, joining the Christian family is beneficial, being held accountable is godly, and properly sharing the biblical narrative is essential. When I joined the United States Army Reserves, I became army property. You are God's property, and you always have been. God loves you so much that He sent His only son, Jesus Christ, to die on the cross to redeem you. This basic training guide was written to help you successfully transform into the person God intended you to be! Get your Bible, a pad, and a pen, and get ready to enjoy the journey.

CHAPTER 1:

Renewing Your Mind Must Be Intentional

"Therefore, I urge you, brothers and sisters, in view of God's mercy, to offer your bodies as a living sacrifice, holy and pleasing to God—this is your true and proper worship. Do not conform to the pattern of this world, but be transformed by the renewing of your mind. Then you will be able to test and ap-prove what God's will is—his good, pleasing and perfect will." (Romans 12:1-2)

Basic training was a necessary process to change me from a civilian to a soldier. The army took specific steps to change my mindset. Likewise, our relationship with God cannot be left up to chance. In Matthew 22:29, Jesus informed the

Sadducees that they were in error because they did not know the Scriptures or the power of God. Jesus went on to share the greatest commandment:

The Greatest Commandment

"Love the Lord your God with all your heart and with all your soul and with all your mind. This is the first and greatest commandment. And the second is like it: Love your neighbor as yourself. All the Law and the Prophets hang on these two commandments." (Matthew 22:37-40)

To fall in love with the Lord, we must spend time fellowshipping with Him. We must develop a lifestyle that includes regularly being in the presence of God. With proper discipleship, we learn the importance of love, so we can begin to love God and our neighbor. We must become people who diligently seek after the presence of God, which comes with a host of rewards as described in the Bible. Like becoming a successful soldier, this behavior is learned but not forced. We must take intentional steps to ensure we read and study the Bible, memorize scriptures, meditate, pray, worship, fast, fellowship with other Christians, be active in a local church, spend time in silence and solitude, serve, and spread the gospel. We cannot be successful as Christians if we do not renew our minds via the Word of God. In this chapter, I will discuss the need for a paradigm shift, how we are impacted by modern culture, and why our response to the cultural pull must be intentional so our lives will glorify God.

To be effective as Christians, we must make a paradigm shift. "The term paradigm shift was introduced by Thomas Kuhn in his highly influential landmark book, *The Structure of Scientific Revolutions*. Kuhn shows how almost every significant breakthrough in the field of scientific endeavors is first a break with tradition, with old ways of thinking, with old paradigms" (Covey, 2015, pp. Kindle Locations

275-277). The Bible spoke of a paradigm shift in Romans 12:1-2 when the apostle Paul urged the saints to be transformed by the renewing of their minds. Paul urges us to offer our bodies as a living sacrifice and directs us not to be conformed to this world but to renew our minds. Paul informs us that presenting our bodies as a living sacrifice is a reasonable requirement. He goes on to say that instead of being conformed to this world, we can experience a transformation in our lives if we renew our minds which moves us to God's good, acceptable, and perfect will. Paul is urging us to change our worldview. Worldview is the framework in which you view the world, your calling, and your future in the world (Sire 2009, Kindle Location 115). Prior to enrolling in seminary, I did not give enough consideration to the impact that modern culture, electronic media, the things we read, and what we watch on television has on our lives. The goal for you is to immediately embrace the need to spend time with the Lord and get to know Him for

4

yourself by studying His Word. Guard your mind by controlling how much time you spend in front of the television or on social media and begin to become the person God intended you to be.

The Impact of Modern Culture

Electronic Media & Books

Today, many Christians are unaware of the major impact that culture has on us. Censorship standards in electronic media have changed a great deal over the past thirty years. Observe how the entertainment industry has increased exposure to more and more sexual content, extreme violence, and foul language. Gradually, Christians have accepted full frontal nudity, rape and sexual abuse of women, X-rated sex scenes, murder scenes, and torture as a normal part of television. Max Anders stated in his book *Brave New Discipleship: Cultivating Scripture-driven Christians in a Culture-driven World,* "Christians must either pull away from modern culture and isolate themselves from electronic media (which is not likely to happen), or they must find ways of offsetting the pervasiveness and power of electronic media" (Anders 2015, p. 5). Although I am not a big television watcher or internet buff, I did not fully consider the impact that electronic media had on me, and how it can impact my level of acceptance of the things of this world.

Electronic media is not the only thing that is impacting our thought processes. Christians must also be aware of the impact of literature. There is a great deal of literature available to captivate the mind of Christian readers. We need to be able to think critically before making the decision to read certain literature. Without the ability to discern and the maturity to understand what one is reading, Christians can be engrossed in a book only to learn that the information they read was contrary to our Christian worldview. In *Lit! A Christian Guide to Reading Books* by Tony Reinke, Reinke identified three types of books that Christians should avoid:

books because of timing (young readers or babes in Christ), books that glorify evil (books that celebrate sin or leave evil unresolved), and books for conscience's sake (books conforming to non-Christian thought patterns) (Reinke 2011). In 2 Corinthians 10:5, we are told to cast down imaginations and every high thing that exalteth itself against the knowledge of God, and to bring into captivity every thought to the obedience of Christ. The goal is to guard our minds and aggressively embrace our Christian worldview.

Worldly Mindset

Myles Munroe once stated that "the mind can be impregnated by ideas that develop into concepts that become visions that produce reality" (Munroe 2004, p. 15). But not every idea is a godly idea. Christians need to realize how much influence modern culture such as electronic media and uncensored books have changed the norms over the years. To combat these changes, as Christians we must take intentional steps to renew our minds. We need to take intentional steps to be that "chosen generation, royal priesthood, holy nation, and peculiar people" that the Bible talks about in 1 Peter 2:9. Marva J. Dawn wrote in her article "How Christian Worship (not Consumerist Worship) Forms a Missional Community" that "the Christian community must be an alternative society—offering its gifts of different ways to think and speak and be and behave to a world that is desperate for them" (Dawn 2000).

As Dawn suggests and the Bible demands, Christians are to be set apart from the world. Romans 8:6-8 states, "For to be carnally minded *is* death; but to be spiritually minded *is* life and peace. Because the carnal mind *is* enmity against God: for it is not subject to the law of God, neither indeed can be. So then they that are in the flesh cannot please God" (KJV). Due to total depravity, we are all born with a carnal mind. Christians must take intentional steps to ensure that we do not have a worldly mindset. "Our wants and longings and desires are at the core of our identity, the wellspring from which our actions and behavior flow" (Smith 2016, Kindle Location 99). These wants flow from deep down in our unconscious being. This is why renewing our mind is so essential. Galatians 6:8 tells us that "For he that soweth to his flesh shall of the flesh reap corruption; but he that soweth to the Spirit shall of the Spirit reap life everlasting" (KJV). The Bible is clear that we are to think on whatsoever things are true, honest, just, pure, lovely, things that are of good report, virtuous, and worthy of praise (Phil. 4:8 KJV). This thought process cannot be just in our conscious mind. The Philippians 4:8 thought process must be deep down in our very core; in our unconscious mind.

Unconscious Results

We were fearfully and wonderfully made (Ps. 139:14) in God's image, but sin defaced God's original plan for our lives. Now, unconsciously our minds are carnal. If we fail to renew our minds, fail to strive to be Christ-like, and are unaware of the impact that modern culture has on us, we will be defeated. Unconsciously, we have formed a lot of bad habits that need to be replaced with good habits. Stephen Covey defines "a habit as the intersection of knowledge, skill, and desire" (Covey 2015, Kindle Locations 580-581). Covey defines knowledge, skill, and desire as follows:

"Knowledge is the theoretical paradigm, the what to do and the why. Skill is the how to do. And desire is the motivation, the want to do. In order to make something a habit in our lives, we have to have all three" (Covey 2015, Kindle Locations 582-583).

A visual of what Covey articulates would look like this:

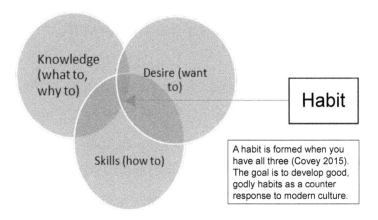

Knowledge (what to, why to)

Desire (want to)

Skills (how to)

Habit

A habit is formed when you have all three (Covey 2015). The goal is to develop good, godly habits as a counter response to modern culture.

James K. A. Smith writes about the spiritual power of habits in his book, *You Are What You Love*. He reminds us not to "ignore the overwhelming power of habits" (Smith 2016, Kindle Location 133). We renew our mind with Scripture, but we also want to replace our worldly habits with Christ-like habits so that we can **instinctively** be like Christ. In order for our Christ-like behavior to become second nature, we must intentionally create new "Christ-like" habits.

My Response to the Cultural Pull

Richard Paul and Linda Elder stated in their book *Miniature Guide to Critical Thinking Concepts & Tools*, that "shoddy thinking is costly, both in money and in quality of life. Excellence in thought, however, must be systematically cultivated" (Paul and Elder 2014, Kindle Locations 31-32). Worldly living and thinking is also costly, both in money and in quality of life. Christ-like thinking and Christ-like living, however, also must be systematically cultivated. We must take intentional steps to study the Word of God, to renew our minds, to become Christ-like, and to do the will of God. Christians sometimes forget that "the Bible was written not to be studied but to change our lives" (Hendricks and Hendricks 1991, p. 31). Renewing our minds requires deliberate actions.

Intentional Practices

"From its beginning the church linked the desire for more of God to intentional practices, relationships, and experiences that gave people space in their lives to 'keep company' with Jesus. These intentional practices, relationships, and experiences we know as spiritual disciplines" (Calhoun 2015, Kindle Location 404-406). "Throughout the centuries the disciplines of prayer, confession, worship, stewardship, fellowship, service, attending to Scripture, and the Lord's Supper have remained constant channels and disciplines of grace. These time-resilient disciplines give the church in every age and culture ways to keep company with Jesus" (Calhoun 2015, Kindle Location 435-438). To keep company with Jesus, Christians must establish a lifestyle of praying, worshiping, meditation, studying the Bible, fasting, and fellowshipping with other Christians to become Christ-like. In an effort "not to live according to the attitudes, values, and behavior of the physical world" (Anders 2015, p. 39) around us but to renew our minds so that we live according to the spiritual world to which God has called us. To do this, we must diligently seek after a relationship with God by making individual worship a habit. I do a good job with corporate worship. I used to do a better job with individual worship, but I let a busy lifestyle effect my individual worship time. I want individual worship to move from my conscious mind to my unconscious mind so that it will just be what I do! I truly enjoy worshiping God both at home and in church. Conforming to my culture, over the past few years my individual worship moved from worshiping God daily to worshiping God three or four times a week. Now, I am intentionally scheduling daily worship in the morning to start my day.

Growing Spiritually

It is God's desire that our whole spirit and soul and body be preserved blameless unto the coming of our Lord Jesus Christ (1 Thess. 5:23). This includes our conscious mind, unconscious mind, our will, and our heart as shown below:

We Are a 3-Part Whole

We are spirit, have a soul and live in a body

(Unknown 2016)

On the contrary, the devil wants to steal, kill, and destroy us; God wants us to live abundantly (John 10:10). Many people are seeking abundant life; unfortunately, we sometimes try to find the abundant life through material items. A big house, an expensive car, and fancy clothes don't equate to abundant life. Tommy Tenney stated in his book *The God Chasers: My Soul Follows Hard after Thee*, "people want to connect with a higher power! Their hunger drives them to everywhere but to God. They search in pursuits of the flesh to try to feed the hunger that gnaws at their souls" (Tenney 1998, 2). Our hunger can only be fed by returning to our first love, God. We do not just want to know about God. We want to have an intimate relationship with Him. We want to be in God's presence and delight in His joy, thus we need to grow spiritually.

At the center of the illustration above is a heart. Anders states that "the pursuit of knowledge is a matter of the heart, not merely of the head" (Anders 2015, p. 58). I would go further and state that obtaining knowledge will impact the whole man. It effects the conscious mind; when we use our knowledge to form new habits, we transform our unconscious minds, exchange our wills for God's will, and we even change our hearts. But it doesn't stop there, knowledge leads to spiritual growth and a healthier mindset. With everything at stake, our relationship with God cannot be left up to chance. We must take intentional steps to ensure we grow in our biblical knowledge. We must take intentional steps to establish a Christ-like lifestyle and grow in our ministry skill.

Smith stated, "We've embraced an 'if-it-feels-good-do-it' rationale that encourages us to 'follow our passions' and act on whatever whim or instinct or appetite moves us" (Smith 2016, Kindle Locations 159). He follows up by stating that this thought process is "why Christians need to focus on thinking— to acquire the knowledge necessary to counter the culture of impulse" (Smith 2016, Kindle Locations 161). We need to spend quality time studying, growing, and learning so we can properly apply the Word of God, renew our minds, and be in God's perfect will.

The military took intentional steps to change our thought processes thus moving us from civilians to successful and committed members of the army family. Training was strategic, consistent, and daily. The military helped to ensure our success by giving us the tools necessary to succeed. Like my military experience, as Christians we need to take strategic, consistent, and daily actions to enhance our success. We need to develop a lifestyle of reading the Bible, meditating, praying, worshiping, fasting, fellowshipping with other Christians, and being active in a local church to move us from a worldly mindset to a Christian worldview. "If any man *be* in Christ, *he is* a new creature" (2 Cor. 5:17). Shouldn't our newness bring about change in our lives? God requires Christians to be holy (Lev. 19:2, 20:7, Eph. 1:4, 1 Pet. 1:16, Josh. 24:19). David Jordan stated, "There is no real excellence in all this world which can be separated from right living" (Covey 2015, 34-35). The apostle Paul talks about that "right living" in Romans 12:1-2 when he urged us to present our bodies as a living sacrifice, holy, acceptable unto God. . .being transformed by the renewing of our minds. Then, it is important that you immediately begin to make that cultural shift. "Old things have passed away; behold, all things have become new" (2 Cor. 5:17) declared the Lord. Begin to walk in your newness. Refuse to say and do what you used to do if it will not please God. A part of the success of army basic training is that you are separated from anything and everything that would be contrary to your success. There may be a time when you need to spend some quiet time studying and growing. When I was working on my Master of Science Degree at Johns Hopkins University, I told my family, friends, job, and church that I had made a two-year commitment to complete this full-time pro-gram. It was important to me and my future. I asked in advance for their understanding and forgiveness because I would be respectfully declining invitations to some events. During that timeframe, I would not be the usual "go-to person" to handle last-minute requests. Instead, I would be limiting my phone calls and would not over extend myself. Why? Because I gleaned the value of completing the program, and I needed to take the steps necessary to ensure my success. I hope you are beginning to see the value in this basic training and are willing to take the steps necessary to ensure your success as a Christian. Johns Hopkins University helped to improve my skill set. Developing a firm foundation by renewing your mind via the Word of God will help transform you, so you will be able to test and prove what God's good, pleasing, and perfect will is for your life.

Chapter Review

1. What is the greatest commandment?

   _____

   _____

   _____

2. _____ is the framework in which you view the world, your calling, and your future in the world.

3. Christians need to _____ how much _____ modern culture such as electronic

media and uncensored books have changed the norms over the years.

4. In an effort to _____ _____ with Jesus, Christians must establish a life-style of _____, _____, meditation, studying the Bible, fasting, and fellowship-ping with other Christians in order to become _____.

5. With everything at stake, our _____ with _____ cannot be left up to chance.

Application

What steps will you take to enhance your relation-ship with God? Which spiritual disciplines do you need to practice more often, and what action are you going to take to improve in these areas?

_____

_____

_____

_____

CHAPTER 2:

Embracing the Theologian Inside You Is Rewarding

For the word of God is alive and active. Sharper than any double-edged sword, it penetrates even to dividing soul and spirit, joints and marrow; it judges the thoughts and attitudes of the heart. Nothing in all creation is hidden from God's sight. Everything is uncovered and laid bare before the eyes of him to whom we must give account. Therefore, since we have a great high priest who has ascended into heaven, Jesus the Son of God, let us hold firmly to the faith we profess. For we do not have a high priest who is unable to empathize with our weaknesses, but we have one who has been tempted in every way, just as we are-yet he did not sin. Let us then approach God's throne of grace with confidence, so that we may receive mercy and find grace to help us in our time of need. (Hebrews 4:12-16)

Although I have been a Christian for many years, for far too long I did not consider myself to be a theologian. Truthfully, I did not have a clear understanding of what theology meant. I have studied the Bible, read some informative Christian books, and attended numerous church seminars; still, I stayed away from that scary word, "theology." The purpose of basic training in the military is to teach recruits everything they need to know to develop a strong military foundation, so they can be successful during their tenure in the military. For soldiers, this foundation will be further developed during AIT and other courses the recruit completes during their career. In Romans 12:1-2, the apostle Paul urges Christians to sacrifice their lives to God by living in a manner described in the Bible. Christians no longer live according to the sin nature, but are to embrace a biblical worldview, being holy and acceptable unto God. Paul explains that we are to be changed by the renewing of our minds to prove God's good, acceptable, and perfect

23

will. To be successful in our Christian faith, we must embrace the theologians we were destined to be by renewing our minds via the Word of God. In this chapter, I will define theology, discuss why all Christians need to be committed to being great theologians, talk about how we can effectively study the Bible, and hopefully spark your interest in becoming a lifelong learner of God's Word.

While in seminary, I discovered that I needed to enroll in the Introduction to Theology, and I was fearful about taking the class. Knowing that "ology" was the study of, I assumed that "theo" meant religion. As much as I love the Lord, I was not excited about what I assumed would be numerous hours learning about branches of religion, the history of religion, etc. Although God has not given us the spirit of fear but a sound mind (2 Tim. 1:7), I dreaded the class. Knowing that part of that sound mind is "thinking on whatever is true" (Phil. 4:8), I decided to find out what the Introduction to Theology class entailed instead of stressing about the unknown. I downloaded my first required reading, *Who Needs Theology? An Invitation to the Study of God* by Stanley J. Grenz and Roger E. Olson and dived right in. Even the title of the book was a clue that I may have the wrong idea of what theology was all about.

As I started my journey of discovery, I did not make it past the first sentence when I discovered that being a Christian and not knowing the definition of theology may be the norm as opposed to the exception when the author stated, "Many Christians today not only are uninformed about basic theology but even seem hostile to it" (Grenz and Olson 1996, Kindle Location 27). Not ready to admit my lack of knowledge, I journeyed on with the thought in my head that this is a book and not a peer reviewed article; other theologians may not agree with Grenz and Olson. I flipped through my kindle for hours and began to discern that the information about theology and the book *Who Needs Theology? An Invitation to the Study of God* was delicious. Yes, I was one of those people who was "hungry for understanding and who may (possibly) offer marvelous insight" (Grenz and Olson 1996, Kindle Location 32) one day. Θεολογία, the Greek word for theology, "comes from a combination of two Greek words: theos, which means God, and logos, which means reason, wisdom or thought. Literally, then, theology means God-thought or reasoning about God" (Grenz and Olson 1996, Kindle Location 68-69). The Oxford Dictionary of the Christian Church defines theology as "the science of God" (Cross and Livingston 2005, 1616). Saint Anselm described theology as *faith seeking understanding* (Williams 2015).

Once I understood what theology meant, it did not seem very scary after all. Now, I needed to have a better understanding of what a theologian was, so I could begin to become the theologian I was meant to be. The Dictionary of Christianity in America defines theologian as "a person who systematically studies theology or some aspect of theology" (Olbricht 1990). According to *Who Needs Theology? An Invitation to the Study of God*, "all Christians may be theologians, but not all theologies are thereby made equal" (Grenz and Olson 1996, Kindle Location 123-124). As a Christian who studies the Bible with a desire to clearly understand, correctly articulate, and effectively apply the Word of God so I can live in accordance to God's will and be a good witness, I am a theologian; but as Grenz and Olson stated, not all theologians are made equal (Grenz and Olson 1996, Kindle Location 123-124). It is my desire to develop into a good theologian, so I can be "salt and light in a world that desperately needs bright, articulate Christians" (Grenz and Olson 1996, Kindle Location 42).

Blessed is the one who does not walk in step with the wicked or stand in the way that sinners take or sit in the company of mockers, but whose delight is in the law of the Lord, and who meditates on his law day and night. That person is like a tree planted by streams of water, which yields its fruit in season and whose leaf does not wither— whatever they do prospers. (Psalm 1:1-3)

As Christians, we must recognize the importance of becoming theologians. We must change
the stereotype about theology and embrace the
need to diligently seek God (Heb. 11:6). Olympic
athletes rise early in the morning to train, commit
many hours a day to perfect their skill, and sacrifice money and lifestyle so they can be the best in
their field. They commit to a strict diet and exercise
routine, miss out on time with family and friends,
and travel around the world to compete. Olympic
athletes have a strong work ethic. They are willing
to do whatever it takes to be recognized as number
one, and they will "diligently pursue" winning the

medal. The reward for diligently seeking God is abundant life on earth (John 10:10) and eternal life thereafter (Rom. 6:23). If an athlete is willing to make such a commitment to win the gold medal, why shouldn't Christians be willing to diligently seek after a relationship with God for the reward of abundant life on earth and eternal life thereafter?

The Bible informs us that if we delight in the law of the Lord and meditate on His law day and night, we will be like a tree planted by the streams of water (Ps. 1:2). Meditation (Greek - μελετή, *meditatio*) is defined as the "recitation or memorizing of scriptures; keeping various religious truths or inspirational thoughts in mind during the day; thinking about things, whether the emphasis is on intellectual rigor, acuteness of perception, or devotional fervor" (Cross and Livingston 2005). Studying and memorizing scriptures is essential for theologians and thus essential if we are going to renew our minds. 2 Corinthians 5:17 states, "Therefore, if anyone is in Christ, the new creation has come: The old has gone, the new is here!" Being a theologian is necessary for every Christian to learn his or her role as a new creation.

Our primary source of studying must be the Bible. All other sources are secondary tools that can enhance our understanding and growth. Early in my Christian walk, I would only refer to the Bible for guidance and direction. Desiring not to "read a verse out of its immediate literary context, its context in light of the whole Bible, or its historical context" (Svigel 2012, Kindle Locations 734-736), I later learned to use tools to enhance my knowledge and understanding of the Word of God. As I began to develop as a critical thinking theologian (still trying to become a good theologian), my basic library grew. Initially, the King James Version (KJV) of the Bible was my primary resource. In an effort to grow, I invested in a New International Version (NIV) Study Bible, the Strongest Strong's Exhaustive Concordance of the Bible, a Bible dictionary, a topical Bible, a Bible handbook, and a good commentary to enhance my understanding. Word study books, maps, and other books written by professional theologians have also proven to be very helpful as I continue to grow. As a Bible study teacher and curriculum writer for my church, it is very important that I thoroughly study the Bible so that I can correctly articulate it to others. Developing into a good theologian means we can enhance our relationship with God, we can determine who God created us to be, and we can better serve others.

My thought process about theology has shifted. We should all be excited about the possibility of one day becoming excellent theologians. We must all study to show ourselves approved, so we can rightly divide the word of truth (2 Tim. 2:15)! Rick Warren stated:

"Studying the Bible is like being a good detective. A good Bible student basically follows the same procedure as a good sleuth. The first thing a detective does is to go out and look for clues. He doesn't say anything, interpret anything, or draw any conclusions, but he does look at all the details" (Warren 1981, Kindle Location 274-276).

As a retired police officer with over twenty-five years of police experience, I have conducted many investigations. All my years of conducting investigations serve me well as I look at the details in the Word of God to help me leave no stone unturned. God desires that we all study the Word of God for ourselves. As an investigator, I enjoyed finding evidence to prove or disprove a suspect's involvement in a crime. Gathering evidence, conducting interviews, running surveillances, examining crime scenes, and analyzing data were all steps necessary to determine what occurred. Just as a detective must take particular steps to solve a crime, theologians must thoroughly and properly study the Word of God. Christians benefit greatly from the work of other seasoned theologians.

Discernment

"The sound judgment which makes possible the distinguishing of good from evil, and the recognition of God's right ways for his people. It is necessary for the understanding of spiritual realities and, on a practical level, for right government and the avoidance of life's pitfalls." (Manser, Dictionary of Bible Themes: The Accessible and Comprehensive Tool of Topical Studies 2009)

Aristotle once stated, "It is the mark of an educated mind to be able to entertain a thought without accepting it." Christian readers can benefit from mastering this skill. With a wealth of literature available to captivate the mind, Christian readers need to be able to critically think about the information they are reading and make a choice if it is something they should put in their spirit. A good book can take us to the Great Pyramid of Giza or make us long for a safari trail in Africa. A scholarly article can spark an idea for a great invention or a powerful movement that can affect positive change in many lives. However, a poorly vetted journal can provide inaccurate information that we can be chewing on for weeks, months, and even years to come. The ability to discern with the maturity to understand what one is reading will prevent a young Christian from wasting valuable time fixated on a book only to learn that the content is wrong, misleading, or contrary to our Christian worldview. We enhance our ability to discern by developing a life of devotion via reading the Bible daily, having a lifestyle of prayer, meditating on the Word of God, worshiping, fasting, fellowshipping with God, and by spending time in His presence. In *Lit! A Christian Guide to Reading Books* Tony Reinke stated, "Developing a biblical worldview is labor-intensive, but the result is a discerning mind that is essential if we will benefit from books" (Reinke 2011, p. 53).

The Great Commission

"Then the eleven disciples went to Galilee, to the mountain where Jesus had told them to go. When they saw him, they worshiped him; but some doubted. Then Jesus came to them and said, "All authority in heaven and on earth has been given to me. Therefore go and make disciples of all nations, baptizing them in the name of the Father and of the Son and of the Holy Spirit, and teaching them to obey everything I have commanded you. And surely I am with you always, to the very end of the age."
(Matthew 28:16-20)

Too often, Christians lack the discipline to learn so we happily live based on folk theology, missing out on that abundant life that God desires for us. Proverbs 2:10-11 states, "For wisdom will enter your heart, and knowledge will be pleasant to your soul. Discretion will protect you, and understanding will guard you." We do not study the Word of God for pure knowledge (1 Cor. 8:1). We study the Word of God so we can know who God is; renew our minds; learn God's testimonies, commandments, and precepts; We learn how to fellowship, praise, and worship God. We learn how to be healthy Christians, learn who we are in Christ Jesus, and learn how to properly do the great commission as Jesus directed us. Like the thorough detective, we need to use all the tools in our "tool box" when studying the Word of God, so we can effectively witness to others. For too long, my perspective led me to overlook the need to use tools other than just the Bible to grow as a Christian. Benefiting from professional theologians via exhaustive concordances, Bible dictionaries, commentaries, and other documents has been a great help in my growth and understanding.

It is God's desire that all Christians become theologians, so we can know and obey His laws. God desires that we know him intimately. Knowing God's laws are so important that the longest chapter in the Bible, Psalm 119, contains "176 verses emphasizing God's precepts, word, laws, commandments or decrees" (Boice 1998). We must develop a lifestyle of studying the Word of God to renew our minds.

Romans 10:17 (KJV) states, "So then faith cometh by hearing, and hearing by the word of God." We must hear the Word of God daily. Like that Olympic athlete trying to win the gold, we must take intentional steps to study the Bible, grow as Christians, and develop a personal relationship with God.

Renewing our minds is critical to our new lives as Christians. It is impossible to become Christ-like if you don't know the Word of God. The Bible is our roadmap to success, and we must have a daily diet of the Word of God to grow. Romans 12:3 tells us that we all have been given a measure of faith. However, our faith was not designed to stay the same size. The reward of embracing the theologian you were created to be is abundant life on earth and eternal life thereafter. So, become that theologian God called you to be!

<u>Chapter Review</u>

1. A theologian is a person who _____
_____ theology or some aspect
of theology.

2. As _____, we must recognize the
importance to becoming _____.

3. _____ and _____ _____ is
essential for theologians and is essential if
we are going to renew our minds (Rom. 12:2).

4. A Study Bible, an _____ _____,
a Bible dictionary, a _____ Bible, a
Bible handbook, and a good commentary
can enhance your understanding of the
Word of God.

5. In *Lit! A Christian Guide to Reading
Books* Tony Reinke stated, "developing
a _____ _____ is labor-intensive, but
the result is a discerning mind that is essential if we will benefit from books" (Reinke
2011, p. 53).

Application

What steps will you take immediately to become the theologian God created you to be? Find someone who will hold you accountable for these steps.

_____

_____

_____

_____

_____

_____

_____

_____

_____

CHAPTER 3:

Recognizing the Power of Prayer Is Uplifting

"If my people, who are called by my name, will humble themselves and pray and seek my face and turn from their wicked ways, then I will hear from heaven, and will forgive their sin and will heal their land."
(2 Chron. 7:14)

According to the Strongest Strong's Exhaustive Concordance of the Bible published in 2001, the word "pray" (or prayed, prayer, prayers, prayest, prayeth, praying) can be found in the Bible 313 times. 1 Thessalonians 5:17 directs us to "Pray without ceasing." Mark 1:35 states, "Very early in the morning, while it was still dark, Jesus got up, left the house and went off to a solitary place, where he prayed." Philippians 4:6-7 states, "Do not be anxious about anything, but in every situation, by prayer and petition, with thanksgiving, present your requests to God. And the peace of God, which transcends all understanding, will guard your hearts and your minds in Christ Jesus." James 5:16 states, "Therefore confess your sins to each other and pray for each other so that you may be healed. The prayer of a righteous person is powerful and effective." Ephesians 6:18 states, "And pray in the Spirit on all occasions with all kinds of prayers and requests. With this in mind, be alert and always keep on praying for all the Lord's people." I can go on and on, but I guess you are beginning to see how important praying is. In this chapter, I will define prayer, discuss how Jesus taught us to pray, discuss how learning the Word of God makes praying easier, and share how the Holy Spirit helps us to develop a lifestyle of prayer.

The Bible provides many examples of the importance of prayer, the benefits of prayer, how to pray, and examples of Jesus praying. As Joseph M.

Scriven wrote in his 1855 song, *What a Friend We Have in Jesus*:

What a friend we have in Jesus,
All our sins and griefs to bear!
What a privilege to carry
Everything to God in prayer!
O what peace we often forfeit,
O what needless pain we bear,
All because we do not carry
Everything to God in prayer.

Jesus set the example of the importance of prayer. We can quickly see that praying is an important part of our basic Christian training and a critical part of developing into who God desires us to be. So, what is prayer and how do we learn to pray? The Concise Oxford English dictionary defines pray and prayer as follows:

"pray"

■ **verb:** address a prayer to God or another deity.

■ **adverb:** formal or archaic used in polite requests or questions.

"prayer"

■ **noun:** a solemn request for help or expression of thanks addressed to God or another deity (Soanes and Stevenson 2004).

It also stated that to not have a prayer is to have no chance or no hope (Soanes and Stevenson 2004). Edwin Keith stated prayer is exhaling the spirit of man and inhaling the Spirit of God (Jones 1986). As we learn to pray the Word of God over our lives, Keith's definition becomes our reality. Prior to committing our lives to the Lord, we did what we wanted to do, when we wanted to, and we suffered the consequences. But as Scriven proclaimed, what a privilege to carry everything to God in prayer. When we pray, we are talking to God. We carry our problems to God. As we grow, we learn to hear from and be guided by the Holy Spirit (We will learn about the Holy Spirit in chapter 4). It is our kingdom privilege to talk to God, and He desires that we have an intimate relationship with Him. Before we can talk about the power in prayer, I want to ensure you know how to pray. In the book of Matthew, Jesus taught the disciples how to pray. Before He taught them, Jesus gave these directions: do not pray to be seen, heard, or glorified by others. When we pray, we need to ensure our motives are correct. We do not have to use fancy words or be repetitive, but we do need to recognize the structure that Jesus used in what we call the Lord's Prayer: "Our Father which art in heaven, Hallowed be thy name. Thy kingdom come, Thy will be done in earth, as it is in heaven. Give us this day our daily bread. And forgive us our debts, as we forgive our debtors. And lead us not into temptation but deliver us from evil: For thine is the kingdom, and the power, and the glory, for ever. Amen" (Matt. 6:9-13 KJV).

Part 1 - Adoring God and recognizing His holiness as we open our prayer: "Our Father which art in heaven, Hallowed be thy name." We start our prayer with words of adoration to God recognizing who He is, how wonderful He is, and how worthy He is to be praised. This is the time to glorify God.

Part 2 - Submitting our will to God, "Thy kingdom come, thy will be done in earth, as it is in heaven." In the Garden of Gethsemane Jesus said, "Father, if you are willing, take this cup from me; yet not my will, but yours be done" (Luke 22:42). Jesus Christ, our Lord and Savior, submitted His will to the will of the Father. We must also submit our will to God.

Part 3 - Recognizing that He supplies all needs: "Give us this day our daily bread." Philippians 4:19 reminds us that God will supply every need according to His riches in glory in Christ Jesus. Our goal is to fully embrace Matthew 6:25-34, and understand that God supplies our needs.

Instead of Worrying, Trust God!

"Therefore I tell you, do not worry about your life, what you will eat or drink; or about your body, what you will wear. Is not life more than food, and the body more than clothes? Look at the birds of the air; they do not sow or reap or store away in barns, and yet your heavenly Father feeds them. Are you not much more valuable than they? Can any one of you by worrying add a single hour to your life? "And why do you worry about clothes? See how the flowers of the field grow. They do not labor or spin. Yet I tell you that not even Solomon in all his splendor was dressed like one of these. If that is how God clothes the grass of the field, which is here today and tomorrow is thrown into the fire, will he not much more clothe you-you of little faith? So do not worry, saying, 'What shall we eat?' or 'What shall we drink?' or 'What shall we wear?' For the pagans run after all these things, and your heavenly Father knows that you need them. But seek first his kingdom and his righteousness, and all these things will be given to you as well. Therefore do not worry about tomorrow, for tomorrow will worry about itself. Each day has enough trouble of its own." (Matthew 6:25-34)

Part 4 - Acknowledging that He forgives our sins thus we forgive others: "And forgive us our debts, as we forgive our debtors." Forgiveness is so important that Jesus stated in Matthew 5:21-26 that we must walk in love and peace with everyone. It is just as important for us to walk in forgiveness as it is for us not to commit murder. Thus, we must resolve our faults with others quickly for unforgiveness separates us from God.

Part 5 - Proclaiming our continuous need of His protection and covering: "And lead us not into temptation but deliver us from evil." This is our opportunity to acknowledge that God will protect us from temptation, evil, fear, troubles, our enemies, etc.

Temptation

- **1 Corinthians 10:13**: "No temptation has overtaken you except what is common to mankind. And God is faithful; he will not

BASIC TRAINING FOR CHRISTIANS

let you be tempted beyond what you can bear. But when you are tempted, he will also provide a way out so that you can endure it."

- **1 Thessalonians 5:23-24**: "May God himself, the God of peace, sanctify you through and through. May your whole spirit, soul and body be kept blameless at the coming of our Lord Jesus Christ. The one who calls you is faithful, and he will do it."

- **Hebrews 2:18**: "Because he himself suffered when he was tempted, he is able to help those who are being tempted."

Evil

- **2 Thessalonians 3:3**: "But the LORD is faithful, and he will strengthen you and protect you from the evil one."

- **Psalm 121:7**: "The LORD will keep you from all harm – he will watch over your life."

Fear

- **Deuteronomy 31:6**: "Be strong and coura-geous. Do not be afraid or terrified because of them, for the LORD your God goes with you; he will never leave you nor forsake you."

- **Isaiah 41:10**: "So do not fear, for I am with you; do not be dismayed, for I am your God. I will strengthen you and help you; I will uphold you with my righteous right hand."

Trouble

- **Psalm 34:19**: "The righteous person may have many troubles, but the LORD delivers him from them all."

- **Psalm 46:1**: "God is our refuge and strength, an ever-present help in trouble."

Enemies

- **Psalm 59:1**: "Deliver me from my enemies, O God; be my fortress against those who are attacking me."

- **2 Samuel 22:3-6**: "My God is my rock, in whom I take refuge, my shield and the horn of my salvation. He is my stronghold, my refuge and my savior - from violent people you save me. 'I called to the LORD, who is worthy of praise, and have been saved from my ene-mies. The waves of death swirled about me; the torrents of destruction overwhelmed me. The cords of the grave coiled around me; the snares of death confronted me.'"

Part 6 - Honoring God as we close our prayer: "For thine is the kingdom, and the power, and the glory, for ever. Amen." This is our opportunity to give God praise. There are many great scriptures to help us develop our praise language. Psalm 95 teaches us to "sing for joy to the Lord. . .shout aloud to the rock of our salvation. . .come before Him with thanksgiving and extol Him.. . .for the Lord is the great God, the great King above all gods. . ..come, let us bow down in worship." Psalm 34:1-8 states, "extol the Lord at all times; His praise will always be on my lips. . .Glorify the Lord with me and let us exalt his name together. . .Taste and see that the Lord is good." Psalm 150:1-3 teaches us to give praise to the Lord, proclaim His name. . .sing praise to Him. . .glory in His holy name. Psalm 98:4-6 states, "Shout for joy to the Lord, all the earth, burst into jubilant song with music; make music to the Lord with the harp, with the harp and the sound of singing, with trumpets and the blast of the ram's horn - shout for joy before the Lord, the King." I enjoy praising God. I challenge you to praise God with the same joy, freedom, and volume that you praise your favorite sports team when they win the super bowl, the world series, or the world cup.

We must pray with the full understanding that it is due to the shed blood of Jesus Christ that we can pray. Hebrews 10:10 states that "We have been made holy through the sacrifice of the body of Jesus Christ once for all." Romans 3:23–24 teaches us that "For all have sinned and fall short of the glory of God, and all are justified freely by his grace through the redemption that came by Christ Jesus." It is because of the shed blood of Jesus Christ that we are righteous. It is not because we did anything to earn it. It is not because we are so articulate, talented, or smart. His grace is made perfect in our weakness (2 Cor. 12:9). "The prayer of a righteous person is powerful and effective" (James 5:16), and our righteousness is a gift from Jesus.

As you develop a lifestyle of reading the Word of God, your ability to pray and praise God will become easier because we pray the Word of God. Another important thing to know about prayer is you should ask God to forgive you of any sins of omission (things we have failed to do) or commission (things we shouldn't have done). We need to ensure we have a clean heart and right spirit (Ps. 51:10). This is needed to ensure that our sins do not block our prayers. We need to pray to God in the name of Jesus (John 14:13-14). We need to pray with the understanding that we have the Holy Spirit who is our advocator (John 14:16-18,26), our guide (John 16:13) and will bring the Word of God to our remembrance (John 14:26). Also, we must have faith when we pray (Heb. 11:6).

To help me get ready for prayer, I like to start with a good worship song or two. Psalm 33:1-3 states, "Sing joyfully to the Lord, you righteous; it is fitting for the upright to praise him. Praise the Lord with the harp; make music to him on the ten-stringed lyre. Sing to him a new song; play skillfully, and shout for joy." Music is powerful and helps to set the tone. You can find songs that you like but a few suggestions are as follows:

- I Worship You Almighty God, There is None Like You
- To Worship You I Live
- Praise Is What I Do
- No Body Greater by VaShawn Mitchell
- Because of Who You Are by Vicki Yohe

Find yourself a prayer partner. One of my best experiences is with my prayer partner Deborah Scott. We met at the gym while trying to work on our physical bodies and ended up praying and studying the Word of God together, which helped us both grow spiritually. The army was big on the buddy system, so when Deborah and I started studying and praying together that was right up my alley. There are so many benefits to having a prayer partner. Matthew 18:19-20 states, "Again, truly I tell you that if two of you on earth agree about anything they ask for, it will be done for them by my Father in heaven. For where two or three gather in my name, there am I with them." There is a direct benefit for Christians to stand in agreement and pray together. Plus, God will be in the midst. Ecclesiastes 4:9-12 (KJV) states:

"Two are better than one; because they have a good reward for their labour. For if they fall, the one will lift up his fellow: but woe to him that is alone when he falleth; for he hath not another to help him up. Again, if two lie together, then they have heat: but how can one be warm alone? And if one prevail against him, two shall withstand him; and a threefold cord is not quickly broken."

Proverbs 27:17 teaches us that "As iron sharpens iron, so one person sharpens another." I experienced this firsthand as Deborah and I studied, prayed, challenged, and helped each other grow.

I highly recommend that every new Christian invest in the book *Prayers That Avail Much* by Germaine Copeland. My aunt, Sandra Ward, who is a true prayer warrior, gave me her old copy of the book. It was barely together, and I had to put some tape on the spine to keep it from totally coming apart. That old raggedy book was so beneficial to my spiritual growth, I had to get a new one. The true power of prayer is seen when we pray the Word of God. John 1:1 teaches us that "In the beginning was the Word, and the Word was with God, and the Word was God." That same "Word became flesh and made His dwelling among us" (John 1:14). "For the word of God is alive and active. Sharper than any double-edged sword, it penetrates even to dividing soul and spirit, joints and marrow; it judges the thoughts and attitudes of the heart" (Heb. 4:12). Thus, we must pray the Word of God. *Prayers That Avail Much* has all types of prayers for all types of situations all based on what the Word of God says about that situation. It will help you enhance your prayer life while helping you to learn the Word of God. After praying, spend some time in silence and wait to hear from God.

With the Holy Spirit inside you, your Bible, your *Prayers That Avail Much* prayer book, a repented heart, faith in God, your favorite worship song, and following Jesus's example, you are ready to develop a powerful prayer life. Now, pray every day. Anything that is truly important to us we schedule time for. Put prayer on your schedule. We say we are too busy to pray but scheduling quiet time to get in the presence of God should be a priority. Pray in the morning when you get up. Pray while you are on your way to work. Pray before you go to bed at night. Pray before you make a major decision. Pray when you are facing a major challenge. Pray before your big test! Pray before you decide on a new career. Pray for your children. Pray for your community. Pray for your government and leaders. Pray for your family and friends. Pray without ceasing (1 Thess. 5:17). The world is depending on the body of Christ, so pray!

Chapter Review

1. We are instructed to pray _____ _____ (1 Thess. 5:17).

2. We need to recognize the structure that Jesus used in what we call the _____ _____ which can be found in Matthew _____.

3. The Lord's Prayer starts with _____ (adoring God and recognizing his holiness) to God.

4. _____ is so important that Jesus states in Matthew 5:21-26 that we must walk in love and peace with everyone.

5. God will protect you from: temptation, _____, _____, troubles, and our _____ (etc., etc.).

6. We must _____ with the full understanding that it is due to the _____ blood of Jesus Christ that enables us to pray.

7. We need to pray with the understanding that we have the _____ _____ who is our counselor (John 14:16-18), our _____ (John 14:26), our guide (John 16:13) and will bring the Word of God to our remembrance (John 14:26).

8. "_____ are better than _____; because they have a good reward for their labor" (Eccles. 4:9-12).

Application

Search the Word of God to find scriptures related to an area you want to pray about. Begin to pray those scriptures over your life. Find a prayer partner. Your prayer partner must be a born-again believer. Your prayer partner must be willing to pray the Word of God. You and your prayer partner must agree to hold each other accountable. You and your prayer partner should keep a journal.

_____

_____

_____

_____

_____

_____

_____

CHAPTER 4:

Knowing the Holy Spirit Is Your Keeper Is Energizing

"And I will ask the Father, and he will give you another advocate to help you and be with you forever- the Spirit of truth. The world cannot accept him, because it neither sees him nor knows him. But you know him, for he lives with you and will be in you. I will not leave you as orphans; I will come to you." (John 14:16-18)

Going away to basic training served many purposes, such as being put in settings that were conducive to learning the army way with limited distractions. Joining the body of Christ is not that way at all. There are many distractions and cultural pulls in our society that attempt to hinder our Christian walk as discussed in Chapter 1. Renewing our minds with the Word of God helps us to know who we are in Christ Jesus. In the Word of God, we learn that before Jesus ascended on high, He left us a comforter, helper, advocate, and guide in the Holy Spirit. In this chapter, I will provide some historical information about the Trinity, so you can better understand the Holy Spirit. Then, I will explain why we should be energized and excited about having the Holy Spirit as our keeper.

During 2017, Apostle Karen Bethea, senior pastor of Set the Captive Free Outreach Center, taught on the Holy Spirit. The ministry focus for the year was: The Most Important Person on the Planet and the scripture was John 14:15-18. The yearly theme was Building a Life of Devotion and the motto was the Holy Spirit is my Keeper!

I cannot thank Pastor Karen enough for the information she provided during the year. I would encourage you to contact Set the Captives Free Outreach Center and get the entire series. Knowing that the Holy Spirit is our keeper is truly energizing. The series includes detailed information on: Who is the Holy Spirit?; the Holy Spirit's function; what the Holy Spirit produces, and what the Holy Spirit is doing now. This series will change your life!

The Trinity

Genesis 1:26 states, "And God said, 'Let us make man in our image, after our likeness: and let them have dominion over the fish of the sea, and over the fowl of the air, and over the cattle, and over all the earth, and over every creeping thing that creepeth upon the earth" (KJV). This was our first indication in the Bible that God is a Triune God. Triune or Trinity means "God exists in three persons and one substance: Father, Son, and Holy Spirit. God is one, yet self-differentiated" (Cross and Livingstone 2005). The word Trinity or the doctrine of the Trinity is not in the Bible. Although there are references in both the Old Testament and the New Testament of the Bible that reveals the Trinity, most evidence can be found in the New Testament. In the next few paragraphs, I will explain the doctrine of the Trinity and each person of the Trinity. I will also include reference scriptures for you to read during your study time.

The New Testament contains 120 Trinitarian passages that reveal the revelation of the Trinity (Humphreys 2006) as proclaimed in the doctrine of the Trinity. The New Testament also provides the clear distinction of the Godhead (Berkhof 1938) with three persons who all have distinct roles. The three persons can be seen in Matthew 3:16-17 (KJV) which states, "And Jesus, when he was baptized, went up straightway out of the water: and, lo, the heavens were opened unto him, and he saw the Spirit of God descending like a dove, and lighting upon him: And lo a voice from heaven, saying, This is my beloved Son, in whom I am well pleased." This scripture reveals the three persons of God: Jesus the Son (who is baptized), the Holy Spirit (descending like a dove), and God the Father (whom is well pleased). This distinction of the Godhead can also be seen again in Matthew 28:16-20 (KJV) when Jesus gave the Great Commission to the disciples. Jesus directed the disciples to baptize "in the name of the Father, and of the Son, and of the Holy Spirit" (Erickson 2013).

The Father, Son, and Holy Spirit are "not identical; they interact with one another and their identities are constituted with respect to one another (Matt. 3:16–17; 12:32; 17:5; Luke 3:21–22; 4:1; John 15:26; 16:7–16; 2 Cor. 13:14)" (Berkhof 1938). "They act distinctly but in concert with one another (Gen. 1:1–3; John 1:1–3; 2 Cor. 4:6; Col 1:15–17; Heb. 1:2–3)" (Meeks 2016). The Trinity has an ontological order: first the Father, second the Son, and third the Holy Spirit (Berkhof 1938). This order does not imply that either Godhead has more power than the other. While there are works that are done by the Trinity, there are also works that are primary to each Godhead. The Bible describes the creation as primarily God the Father's role (Berkhof 1938) as seen in Ephesians 3:9, "And to make all men see what is the fellowship of the mystery, which from the beginning of the world hath been hid in God, who created all things by Jesus Christ" (KJV). Redemption is primarily God the Son's role as seen in Ephesians 1:1-7 when Paul explains to the saints at Ephesus that we have been chosen before the foundation of the world, predestined to be holy, and we have redemption through the blood of Jesus Christ. Sanctification is primarily the role of the Holy Spirit (Berkhof 1938) as seen in 1 Corinthians 6:11, "But you were washed, you were sanctified, you were justified in the name of the Lord Jesus Christ and by the Spirit of our God."

As we've seen, the Trinity is one divine essence in three persons: Father, Son, and Holy Spirit. "Christian salvation comes from the Trinity, happens through the Trinity, and brings us home to the Trinity" (Sanders 2010). Although the Trinity works together in unity, they are not identical and have some distinct roles. Each member of the Godhead is equal in power and equal in deity.

Jesus Preparing His Disciples for His Crucifixion

In John 14:1-7, Jesus tells the disciples that He is going away. He proclaims,

"Do not let your hearts be troubled. You believe in God; believe also in me. My Father's house has many rooms; if that were not so, would I have told you that I am going there to prepare a place for you? And if I go and prepare a place for you, I will come back and take you to be with me that you also may be where I am. You know the way to the place where I am going. Thomas said to Him, Lord, we don't know where you are going, so how can we know the way? Jesus answered, I am the way and the truth and the life. No one comes to the Father except through me. If you really know me, you will know my Father as well. From now on, you do know him and have seen him."

Throughout the next few chapters, Jesus begins to explain the benefits of the Holy Spirit and advises that the Holy Spirit cannot come until he ascends.

The Holy Spirit as Our Keeper

In John 16:6-15, Jesus was preparing His disciples for His crucifixion. Jesus explained that He was going away but was sending them the **Advocate**, the **Spirt of Truth** who would guide us to all truth and tell us what is yet to come.

"Rather, you are filled with grief because I have said these things. But very truly I tell you, it is for your good that I am going away. Unless I go away, the Advocate will not come to you; but if I go, I will send him to you. When he comes, he will prove the world to be in the wrong about sin and righteousness and judgment: about sin, because people do not believe in me; about righteousness, because I am going to the Father, where you can see me no longer; and about judgment, because the prince of this world now stands condemned. I have much more to say to you, more than you can now bear. But when he, the Spirit of truth, comes, he will guide you into all the truth. He will not speak on his own; he will speak only what he hears, and he will tell you what is yet to come. He will glorify me because it is from me that he will receive what he will make known to you. All that belongs to the Father is mine. That is why I said the Spirit will receive from me what he will make known to you."

As a human father desires to give his children good gifts, God provided us a wonderful gift in the Holy Spirit (Luke 11:13). It is because we have the Holy Spirit as our keeper that we can be successful in our Christian walk. I am excited to advise that the Holy Spirit is the gift that keeps on giving. The Bible teaches about the many gifts that come from the Holy Spirit:

1.	The Holy Spirit is the advocate given to help us.	John 14:16
2.	The Holy Spirit will be with us forever.	John 14:16
3.	The Holy Spirit is the Spirit of Truth.	John 14:17
4.	The world cannot accept the Holy Spirit.	John 14:17
5.	The Holy Spirit lives with us and in us.	John 14:17
6.	The Holy Spirit teaches and reminds us of the Word of God.	John 14:26
7.	The Holy Spirit would not come unless Jesus went away.	John 16:7
8.	The Holy Spirit will guide us to all truth.	John 16:13

9.	The Holy Spirit will tell us what is yet to come.	John 16:13
10.	We learn biblical truths through the Holy Spirit.	John 16:14
11.	We receive power through the Holy Spirit.	Acts 1:8
12.	The Holy Spirit instructs.	Acts 13:2
13.	The Holy Spirit warns.	Acts 20:23
14.	The Holy Spirit helps us in our weakness.	Romans 8:26
15.	The Holy Spirit intercedes for us.	Romans 8:26
16.	The Holy Spirit gives us hope.	Romans 15:13
17.	Our bodies are the temple of the Holy Spirit.	1 Corinthians 6:19
18.	The Holy Spirit can be grieved.	Ephesians 4:30
19.	The Holy Spirit does not make us timid.	2 Timothy 1:7
20.	The Holy Spirit gives us power, love and self-discipline.	2 Timothy 1:7

Praise be to God, before Jesus ascended on high, He provided a helper in the Holy Spirit. It is through the Holy Spirit that we can indeed be successful in our walk. In Galatians 5:16-26, the apostle Paul instructs us to walk by the Spirit and not to satisfy our desires in the flesh:

"So I say, walk by the Spirit, and you will not gratify the desires of the flesh. For the flesh desires what is contrary to the Spirit, and the Spirit what is contrary to the flesh. They are in conflict with each other, so that you are not to do whatever you want. But if you are led by the Spirit, you are not under the law. The acts of the flesh are obvious: sexual immorality, impurity and debauchery; idolatry and witchcraft; hatred, discord, jealousy, fits of rage, selfish ambition, dissensions, factions and envy; drunkenness, orgies, and the like. I warn you, as I did before, that those who live like this will not inherit the kingdom of God. But the fruit of the Spirit is love, joy, peace, forbearance, kindness, goodness, faithfulness, gentleness and self-control. Against such things there is no law. Those who belong to Christ Jesus have crucified the flesh with its passions and desires. Since we live by the Spirit, let us keep in step with the Spirit. Let us not become conceited, provoking and envying each other."

For "the mind governed by the flesh is death, but the mind governed by the Spirit is life and peace" (Rom. 8:6).

The army provided us with tools that are necessary to be successful in one's military career during basic training, but there were no guarantees. There are many great guarantees that Jesus provides us via the Holy Spirit. The Holy Spirit is our advocator and help in a time of need. The Holy Spirit will guide and instruct us. The Holy Spirit will help us recall the Word of God as well as learn biblical truths. Unlike a potential buddy, the Holy Spirit will never leave nor forsake us. The Holy Spirit does not make us timid but gives us hope. We receive power via the Holy Spirit. We must remember that our bodies are the temple of the Holy Spirit and be sure not to grieve Him. When we don't know what to pray, He will guide us. When we don't understand, He will enlighten us. When we don't know which way to go, He will direct us. How exciting is it to know that before Jesus ascended on high, He left us a comforter; praise God for the Holy Spirit!

Chapter Review

1. In the _____ of God, we learn that before Jesus ascended on high, He left us a _____, helper, advocator and guide in the _____ _____.

2. Genesis 1:26 was our first indication in the Bible that God is a Triune _____.

3. The word _____ or the _____ of the Trinity is not in the Bible. Although there are references in both the Old Testament and the New Testament of the Bible that reveals the Trinity, most

evidence can be found in the _____

_____.

4. Jesus explained that He was going away, but He was sending us the _____, the _____ of _____ who will guide us to all truth and tell us what is yet to come.

5. We receive _____through the Holy Spirit.   Ephesians 3:16-17

6. The Holy Spirit is the _____ of _____.   John 14:17

7. The Holy Spirit _____ and _____ us of the Word of God.   John 14:26

8. The Holy Spirit will tell us what is _____ to _____.   John 16:13

9. We learn biblical truths _____ the Holy Spirit.   John 16:14

10. The Holy Spirit can be _____.
                    Ephesians 4:30

Application

How do you see your life changing since you enhanced your knowledge about the Holy Spirit?

_____

_____

_____

_____

CHAPTER 5:

Joining the Christian Family Is Beneficial

"Therefore, brothers and sisters, since we have confidence to enter the Most Holy Place by the blood of Jesus, by a new and living way opened for us through the curtain, that is, his body, and since we have a great priest over the house of God, let us draw near to God with a sincere heart and with the full assurance that faith brings, having our hearts sprinkled to cleanse us from a guilty conscience and having our bodies washed with pure water. Let us hold unswervingly to the hope we profess, for he who promised is faithful. And let us consider how we may spur one another on toward love and good deeds, not giving up meeting together, as some are in the habit of doing, but encouraging one another—and all the more as you see the day approaching." (Hebrews 10:19-25)

When I joined the army, I was attracted to the premise that I had joined an elite group of men and women who had met the criteria to unite with this exclusive group. This group had spent many weeks training to protect their country. They did more before eight in the morning than most people did all day! This group soon became one big family with members all over the United States. The connection was even greater if you had attended a specialty school such as airborne or ranger school. If I went anywhere in the United States displaying my jump wings I earned after completing airborne school and ran into a fellow soldier who had been to airborne school, there was an instant connection.

When we dedicate our life to Christ, we become a member of a family much bigger than the army. Joining the Christian family does not require meeting special criteria to gain membership because the price was already paid by Jesus on Calvary. Ephesians 2:8-9 tells us that "For it is by grace you have been saved, through faith—and this is not from yourselves, it is the gift of God—not by works, so that no one can boast." Unlike basic training or airborne school, we did not have to complete the training to ensure our membership. We are saved by the grace of God through the shed blood of Jesus Christ. In this chapter, I will discuss some of the benefits of joining the Christian family.

John 3:16 tells us that "For God so loved the world that he gave his one and only Son, that whoever believes in him shall not perish but have eternal life." We have been grafted into the body of Christ. Jesus described the body of Christ in the parable of the mustard seed in Matthew 13:31-32, "The kingdom of heaven is like a mustard seed, which a man took and planted in his field. Though it is the smallest of all seeds, yet when it grows, it is the largest of garden plants and becomes a tree, so that the birds come and perch in its branches." There are members of the body of Christ all over the world, spreading the gospel and doing the work of the ministry.

In August 2015, thanks to financial support from the Mid Atlantic Association of Women in Law Enforcement (MAAWLE), LTC Janet Prall of the 200th Military Police Command, and the Howard County Police Department, I had the opportunity to go to Cardiff, Wales to celebrate the 53rd Annual International Association of Women Police (IAWP) Training Conference as well as the 100th year of women police in the United Kingdom. One day during lunch break, after I thanked God for what appeared to be a tasty lunch, a lady approached with her plate in hand. She introduced herself as Uzo Iwobi and asked if she could join me. Before she could barely sit down, she replied, "You must be a member of the body of Christ." I responded "yes" and asked what brought her to that conclusion. She stated that I was praying too long to not be part of the family. We both laughed and began to converse. As we prepared to embark on the second half of the training day, another conference attendee approached and asked how long we had known each other. When we explained that we had just met, she was taken aback stating that from the continuous laughter coming from our table, she thought we had been friends for years. Uzo and I laughed again as we proceeded to our class. That was the start of several days of laughter, fellowship, and good old Christian fun.

Uzo, was originally from Africa and was residing in the United Kingdom where she worked as an attorney for a police department. She and I were sisters in Christ residing in different continents serving the same Lord and Savior, Jesus Christ. We shared stories of our respective families; we ate every meal together during the rest of the conference, and she even showed me around Cardiff after hours. As we fellowshipped, I couldn't stop thinking about that parable of the mustard seed Jesus described in Matthew 13:31-32. Although I was the only one from my agency who travelled from Maryland to Cardiff, Wales to attend a conference, God allowed me to link up with another member of the body of

Christ to make my travels more relaxing. Uzo was a strong sister in Christ! She loved the Lord, loved her husband, and couldn't stop talking about how proud she was of her son and daughter. Meeting her truly enhanced my conference experience. But it was not just Uzo's fun loving personality and Christ-like behavior that made meeting her such a joy. It was because God created us to be with other members of the body of Christ.

Ecclesiastes 4:9-12 explains that two are better than one and a cord of three strands is not quickly broken. There is power in unity. For example, when a Christian man and a Christian woman become one, they have a built-in prayer partner. Matthew 18:19 states, "Again, truly I tell you that if two of you on earth agree about anything they ask for, it will be done for them by my Father in heaven." Proverbs 18:22 states, "He who finds a wife finds what is good and receives favor from the LORD." Jesus sent out His disciples in twos (Luke 10:1). When we were sinners, we were self-centered and thought we did not need others, so we have the tendency to separate ourselves from other members of the body of Christ, especially when we make mistakes, feel sad, or are going through rough times. This is just the opposite of what we should do. God created us to help each other, strengthen each other, pray for each other, and love each other.

In December 2016, I wrote and copyrighted a poem for my fitness instructor, Mrs. Ernestine Shepherd (Ms. Ernie as we call her). In 2010 and 2011, Ms. Ernie was the oldest female body builder in the world and was recognized by the Guinness Book of World Records for her achievements. She has won numerous trophies, medals, and awards for her fitness efforts. Her fitness journey started when she was fifty-six and her sister, Mildred Velvet Hawkins, was fifty-seven. Mildred motivated Ms. Ernie to start exercising and later encouraged her to motivate others to eat right, exercise, and drink plenty of water. Ms. Ernie began to see this endeavor as their mission, but Mildred quickly informed Ms. Ernie that it was their ministry. Before long, the sisters had developed a plan, come up with a uniform, and created their own mantra, "Determined, Dedicated and Disciplined to Be Fit" (Shepherd 2016).

Unfortunately, shortly after developing the mantra, Mildred died of a brain aneurysm. To honor the journey Mildred was so committed to, Ms. Ernie has faithfully maintained a lifestyle of fitness ever since. She has been featured in numerous magazines and television shows to include *Good Morning America*, *Essence Magazine,* and *Little Big Shots: Forever Young.* Ms. Ernie has traveled throughout the United States and abroad promoting the need for a healthy lifestyle and to raise awareness about brain aneurysms. She published her first book recently, *Determined, Dedicated, Disciplined to be Fit.* I had only been attending her classes for a few months when I observed that Ms. Ernie, who is now eighty-two years old, was having a major impact on the lives of many. I thought my poem was fitting to explain how being part of a community is critical.

Ernestine "A True" Shepherd

Rising early in the morning she starts out her day.
  Devotions, a healthy breakfast, then quickly
  on her way.
"Determined, dedicated, disciplined to be fit!"
  The lifestyle of a winner she faithfully
  commits.

Working out like a great athlete, all before class.
  Running, lifting weights, and building body mass.
"Now time to get started," in her sweet quiet voice she will say.

On your mats, on your back, settle down
now and lay.

Stretching, crunches, and leg lifts are just a
small part.
For words of wisdom and love does flow
from her heart.
Helping others to embrace a healthy lifestyle you
will clearly see.
But her ability to create a community is what
stood out to me.

Like other shepherds, she protects and cares for
her sheep.
While motivating and encouraging, the room
she will sweep.
"Dedication is the key to success," she will
often declare.
Keep moving, eat right, drink water, she
shares.

"Age is nothing but a number" you'll most likely hear.

Stay committed, don't quit, you know I do care!

"You are my sunshine; you make me happy," she ends.

Her ministry, replacing obesity with healthy new friends!

I am not sure if Ms. Ernie realized the impact she was having on her class, but it was not just about exercise. Ms. Ernie had formed a community. She was leading her sheep by example. She was protecting them, training them, guiding them, and even praying for them. Ms. Ernie is an example of a shepherd who operates outside of the four walls of the church. Her ministry of promoting exercise, eating right, and a healthy lifestyle was also promoting fellowship. She was helping people to connect with others while being committed to a worthwhile cause. Something else I discerned while in the class was that several people were lonely and lacked healthy relationships prior to joining the class. Ms. Ernie had provided a safe haven and a purpose. Via her exercise class, Ms. Ernie became the conduit for the creation of a cord of many strands that will not be easily broken. Hezekiah Walker said it well in his song, "I Need You to Survive," I need you, you need me. We're all a part of God's body" (Walker 2011). He ends the songs stating, "I love you, I need you to survive. It is his will, that every need be supplied. You are important to me, I need you to survive" (Walker 2011).

The thought process in Hezekiah Walker's song is contrary to the way we did things before we became members of the body of Christ; however, we must remember we are in the world but not of the world (John 17:13-16). The Bible states, "For in him we live and move and have our being" (Acts 17:28) so Christ should be at the center of everything we do. When we join the Christian family, we move from independence to intra dependent; we are dependent on the Triune God (the Father, the Son and the Holy Spirit) as well as other members of the body of Christ. There is one body with many functions. We each have a role to play and are needed for the body to function as God intended it to function (Rom. 12:4-5, 1 Cor. 12:27). I need you, you need me, and we are all part of God's body. When embracing our role in the body of Christ or in our new Christian family, we must use a biblical worldview.

Chapter Review

1. There are members of the _____ of _____ all over the world, spreading the gospel and doing the work of the _____.

2. _____ 4:9-12 explains that two are better than one and a cord of three strands is not quickly broken.

3. God created us to _____ each other, _____ each other, _____ for each other and _____ each other.

4. The Bible states, "For in _____ we _____ and _____ and have our being" (Acts 17:28) so Christ should be at the center of everything we do.

5. We each have a _____ to _____ and are needed for the body to function as God intended it to function.

Application

Considering your talent and passion, how can you do your part to contribute to God's will being done?

_____

_____

_____

_____

_____

_____

_____

_____

_____

CHAPTER 6:

Being Held Accountable Is Godly

It is written: "As surely as I live," says the Lord, "every knee will bow before me; every tongue will acknowledge God." So then, each of us will give an account of ourselves to God. (Romans 14:11-12)

One of the greatest things I learned during my time in the army was the importance of being accountable. Army basic training taught me how to appreciate, respect, and recognize the benefit of being held accountable. It was during basic training that my thought process about accountability began to shift. One of the first things you learn in basic training is the three general orders. Although I have been retired from the army for many years now, I still can recite my **Three General Orders**:

First General Order

"I will guard everything within the limits of my post and quit my post only when properly relieved."

Second General Order

"I will obey my special orders and perform all of my duties in a military manner."

Third General Order

"I will report violations of my special orders, emergencies, and anything not covered in my instructions, to the commander of the relief."

These general orders helped me be account-able for my post, my special orders, and any emergencies therein. Accountability is a skill that has helped me throughout my life. Synonyms for accountability include responsibility, answerability, liability, and culpability. When I began to understand the benefits of being held accountable, I became the person that the military could rely upon to get the job done. It was then that I began to progress in the military. The more I mastered accountability, the more the army was willing to invest in me, trust in me, and give me greater responsibilities. Our relationship with God is the same way. The Bible tells us in Romans 14:10-12 that we will all stand before God and be held accountable. To be held accountable to God's will, we must know God's Word. The more we hold ourselves accountable to the will and Word of God, the more successful our lives will be. In this chapter, I will discuss the necessity of being held accountable to God, being held accountable to a pastor, and the requirement of stewardship.

Today, there seems to be a lack of accountability. This lack of accountability is seen in the community, the workplace, the home, and, believe it or not, even the church. We say we love God but do not feel the need to love our neighbor. We say we love God but do not see the need to attend church. We say we love God but do not see the need to submit to a pastor. We state we are Christians, but there is no visible fruit attached with that self-imposed description.

Throughout the Bible, there are references to us being accountable to the Word of God but none more direct than Psalm 119. As discussed in chapter 2, Psalm 119 tells us to know God's laws, ordinance, testimonies, commandments, decrees, precepts, and his statutes. With 179 verses and 315 lines, Psalm 119 has a running accountability theme. Army basic training taught me to live and breathe accountability, which helped to shape my military career. In Psalm 119, I learned the need to live and breathe the Word of God which helped to change my life. Every Christian must learn God's will for their life and develop an intimate relation-ship with God. The foundation of our relationship with God is built on the Word of God and being obedient to the Word of God. The foundation or the groundwork for our new worldview is developed by complying with the Word of God.

When I first contemplated joining the military, a friend and I were joining together in what was termed "the buddy system." The buddy system meant that this new endeavor I was embarking on would not be as scary because I would be going to basic training with someone I knew, cared for, and could confide in. My buddy and I would be together, look out for each other, and would have each other's back. We would be there to offer words of encouragement, cheering each other on during road marches, physical fitness tests, and whatever challenges we would face. We would hold each other accountable for completing assignments, remind each other of the purpose of persevering during those tough times, and, most of all, we would never be alone. This concept did not start with the military. Ecclesiastes 4:9-12 states:

"Two are better than one,

because they have a good return for their labor:

If either of them falls down,

one can help the other up.

But pity anyone who falls

and has no one to help them up.

Also, if two lie down together, they will keep warm.

But how can one keep warm alone?

Though one may be overpowered,

two can defend themselves.

A cord of three strands is not quickly broken."

As I stated in the previous chapter, there is a direct benefit for Christians standing in agreement, studying, and growing together. Like the buddy system in the military, Ecclesiastes 4:9-12 articulates the benefit of working and serving with a friend. Solomon states that two have a larger profit than one alone. He goes on to acknowledge that they can help each other both physically and emotionally when needed, and he offers a level of protection in numbers. He closes with the fact that a third friend would be even better. I sometimes think of Ecclesiastes 4:9:12 as instructions for the Christian Buddy System. The Christian Buddy System means you will have a likeminded person looking out for and holding you accountable.

Being accountable to God means that I read the Word of God, so I am learning His precepts and concepts. Being accountable to God means I am living a holy lifestyle that is pleasing to God inside and outside the church building. Being accountable to God means I am giving of my time, talent, and treasury. Being held accountable to God means I cannot do everything I did before I was saved. John 12:26 states, "Whoever serves me must follow me; and where I am, my servant also will be. My Father will honor the one who serves me." There are many people who identify themselves as Christians but do not read and obey the Word of God. As I stated in chapter 1, basic training was a necessary pro-cess to change me from a civilian to a soldier. We must take intentional steps to ensure we read and study the Bible, memorize scripture, meditate, pray, worship, fast, fellowship with other Christians, be active in a local church, spend time in silence and solitude, serve, and spread the gospel. These are all a part of being accountable to God.

We Are Made Righteousness through Faith and the Shed Blood of Jesus Christ

Romans 3:21-31 states:

"But now apart from the law the righteousness of God has been made known, to which the Law and the Prophets testify. This righteousness is given through faith in Jesus Christ to all who believe. There is no difference between Jew and Gentile, for all have sinned and fall short of the glory of God, and all are justified freely by his grace through the redemption that came by Christ Jesus. God presented Christ as a sacrifice of atonement, through the shedding of his blood—to be received by faith. He did this to demonstrate his righteousness, because in his forbearance he had left the sins committed beforehand unpunished— he did it to demonstrate his righteousness at the present time, so as to be just and the one who justifies those who have faith in Jesus. Where, then, is boasting? It is excluded. Because of what law? The law that requires works? No, because of the law that requires faith. For we maintain that a person is justified by faith apart from the works of the law. Or is God the God of Jews only? Is he not the God of Gentiles too? Yes, of Gentiles too, since there is only one God, who will justify the circumcised by faith and the uncircumcised through that same faith. Do we, then, nullify the law by this faith? Not at all! Rather, we uphold the law."

We were made holy through the sacrifice of the body of Jesus Christ once for all (Heb. 10:10). Now it is our responsibility to change our worldview. It is our responsibility to learn what being a Christian really means. We cannot just be Christians in title only! We must renew our minds and become Christ-like.

On an episode of Potter's Touch, Bishop T.D. Jakes summed it up perfectly when he said, "Did Jesus come and dwell amongst us for thirty-three years, get beat with a cat o' nine tails, stripped of his clothing, nailed to a cross for you to be a church person who still lives in sin?" Bishop Jakes went on to say, "I hear you talk about you're saved but I wonder what you are saved from if you are going to live like you lived before?" The world is depending on the body of Christ to bring healing to the land, but that requires us to humble ourselves, pray, seek

God's face, and turn from our wicked ways. God will hold us accountable to renew our minds.

Accountability in the Bible

The Bible tells us that every careless word we speak, we shall give an account for it in the day of judgment (Matt. 12:36). It tells us that everyone should not be teachers because teachers will be judged by a higher standard and with greater severity, thus we assume the greater accountability and the more condemnation (James 3:1). It teaches us that the more things are given to you, the more actions are required of you (Luke 12:48). There will be a time when we all stand before the throne and give account for our deeds (Rev. 20:12). Hebrews 10:25 directs us not to forsake our own assembling together. John 14:23-24 states, "Jesus replied, 'anyone who loves me will obey my teaching. My Father will love them, and we will come to them and make our home with them. Anyone who does not love me will not obey my teaching. These words you hear are not my own; they belong to the Father who sent me.'"

These are just a few examples of God's requirement of accountability.

Being Accountable to a Pastor

Once we master being accountable to God's will via the Word of God, it is easier to be accountable to a pastor. Hebrews 13:17 states, "Have confidence in your leaders and submit to their authority, because they keep watch over you as those who must give an account. Do this so that their work will be a joy, not a burden, for that would be of no benefit to you." Every Christian would greatly benefit from having a church home and being accountable to a pastor. I could not imagine being a babe in Christ and not having the covering of a pastor. I went to Kingdom First Ministries (KFM) for many years where Drs. Mark and Michelle Holland were the pastors. It was there where Drs. Mark and Michelle began to stretch me, challenge me, and hold me accountable. I could not have had better account-ability partners. Both Drs. Mark and Michelle were veterans. They too had benefited from the military training and discipline. I remember when Dr. Mark called me out of my comfortable seat and asked me to pray. In obedience, I nervously proceeded to the front, quickly said a prayer, and rushed back to my seat. But before that next Sunday, I prayed and prayed at home, so I would feel more prepared to pray, just in case I was asked to pray again. Dr. Mark was teaching me firsthand the need to always be ready or prepared to serve.

Drs. Mark and Michelle taught me the need to have a regular prayer life, to serve in church, to use my gifts for the benefit of the body of Christ, to tithe, and so much more. They covered me and other members of the church in prayer. As I developed and took on more responsibilities in the church, they held me accountable all the more. Ironically, the two seem to go hand in hand. I studied, prayed, worshipped, and fellowshipped with God to be better prepared for whatever assignment my pastors would give me. Because I spent time in preparation, my pastors felt that I was capable, or at least willing, to take on any assignment. Once I learned that my willingness to be held accountable coupled with the fact that God's strength was made perfect in my weakness, I began to feel more comfortable serving in church. My experience at KFM served as a training ground for service in my current church, Set the Captives Free Outreach Center (STCFOC).

Now fellowshipping at STCFOC under the leadership of Pastors Linwood and Dr. Karen Bethea, I continue to embrace accountability. When I first started attending STCFOC in 2012, I felt a little overwhelmed. STCFOC is a large church. As a natural introvert who had attended a small church for the previous twelve years or so, joining STCFOC was a challenge. The challenge was only due to the size because I absolutely love STCFOC. I love the quality Scripture-based preached word that Pastor Karen and other leaders provide. I love the guidance and atmosphere that Pastors Linwood and Karen Bethea provide. I love our "Dream Team" of core leaders who all offer different gifts and talents that ultimately help to make a well-rounded whole!

All this was evident to me quickly when I started attending the church, but being the introvert that I am, it was still a challenge by the mere size of the church. At STCFOC, the Eagles (our awesome Security Ministry) will direct you where to sit. The first few months, I set on any side, any row, with anybody. The problem with this is, it is hard to get to know anyone, and it is easy to not show up, because if you don't know anyone, your church members will not be in your Christian Buddy System. I quickly realized that I needed to be strategic in where I sat. This was not to take ownership of a seat but rather to help with my self-appointed accountability and to get to know others in the church. See, when I randomly sat anywhere; front, back, left, or right;

I noticed that for months people would hug and welcome me like I was a first-time visitor. I had not joined any ministry yet and had not even officially joined the church, so that was the first time they had seen me; in their minds, I was new.

When I started sitting on the same side of the church in the same area, if I had to work on a Sunday, the next Sunday, the cute little elderly lady would give me a hug and say, "I did not see you last week." Before I knew it, I had been grafted into my own little small community within the larger community. Joining what I call the Christian Buddy System proved to be very helpful. Due to the use of technology, the Christian Buddy System is more advanced than when I joined the army. Within minutes, my Christian Buddy System can ensure that I made it safely home from an evening out, spread the word and begin to pray when I am sick, invite me out for an evening in Annapolis for some much-needed fellowship, and even chastise me in love when they discover I am going through something and failed to reach out for prayer.

Another area of accountability that comes with joining a church is actively participating in Bible study. We can and should study the Bible at home, but there is a great benefit to attending Bible study especially when we are babes in Christ. The Bible is made up of sixty-six books that are divided into two sections; The Old Testament (or Covenant) with thirty-nine books, and the New Testament with twenty-seven books written by at least forty authors with no contradiction. The Old Testament contains law, history, poetry, and major and minor prophets. The New Testament contains the gospels, history, Paul's letters to the Church, Paul's letter to friends, and general letters. It was written in Hebrew, Aramaic, and Greek by diverse authors, but all inspired by God. There is a lot to learn about the Bible, so basic training for Christians must include attending and being committed to a structured Bible study program.

I love the quality Scripture-based Bible study that is offered at STCFOC via our PATH program. PATH stands for Pointing All Towards Heaven and is not limited to just studying the Bible but is indicative of the church's mission: "to fill people so full of the Word of God that it liberates every area of their lives spirit, soul and body." So, if you get on the PATH, you can study the Word of God and you can enroll in numerous spiritual enrichment classes that include but are not limited to the following:

Foundational / Prerequisites

- New Members Class
- What We Believe
- Walking in Victory Part I
- Walking in Victory Part II
- Walking in Victory Part III
- Growing into Wholeness

Spiritual Enrichment

- How to Study the Bible
- Leadership Institute
- Ministry of the Holy Spirit
- Confusing Bible Passages
- Walking Out Forgiveness
- God's Will for my Gifts
- Prayer & Fasting
- Topical
- Personal Sanctification

Special Interest

- ABC Kids
- Next Gen
- Joshua's Journey
- Election Process
- Understanding the Political Process
- Photography
- War Room
- Cooking
- Home Improvement for Women
- Single Women Raising Sons
- Entrepreneurship
- Interior Decorating
- The Absent Father Syndrome

Educational Needs

- Tionna Bladon Expanded (Preparing of College)
- Assistance with Adult Education
- How to complete a Free Applicaiton for Federal Student Aid (FAFSA)
- How to Earn an Assoicates Degree and your High School Diploma simutantously
- How to Complete a College Application
- Dealing with the Scholarship Process

Social Needs

- Pre-martial Guidance
- Love and Respect
- Life After Series. . . .
- Dealing with Domestic Violence/ Breakup Violence
- How to Respond to Police
- Family Clinic
- How to Enjoy the Millennial Generation
- Dealing with the Blended Family
- How to use Social Media Safely
- Responding to Cyber Bullying/ Bullying
- Wife Classes
- Husband Classes

Health / Physical Fitness

- Healing Clinic
- Nutrition:Healthy Eating & Healthy Cooking
- Annually Required Health Screening for Men & Women
- How to Grow Your Own Food
- Smoothie Making Class
- Exercise Classes
- Recovering from Surgery
- Cleansing

Financial Stability

- Developing a Sound Mind
- Dealing with Stress
- Mental Health Services
- Care for the Care Taker
- Suffering
- Understanding Depression
- Partnerships
- Grandparents Raising Grandchildren

Financial Stability

- Financial Clinic
- Budgeting
- Retirement Planning
- Life Insurance/ Health Insurance
- Investing
- Estate Planning
- Grant Writing
- Medicare, Medicaid, and AARP
- Buying a Home
- Government, VA, and Other Programs

At STCFOC, Pastors Linwood and Dr. Karen want to ensure that people enjoy the abundant life that Jesus promised here on earth and then enjoy eternal life with the Father once you leave this earth. Basic training for Christians must include a regular diet of the Word of God. Aristotle stated, "We are what we repeatedly do. Excellence, then, is not an act, but a habit." I cannot say it enough, Christians must make studying, reflecting on, and applying the Word of God a habit, which is a form of accountability.

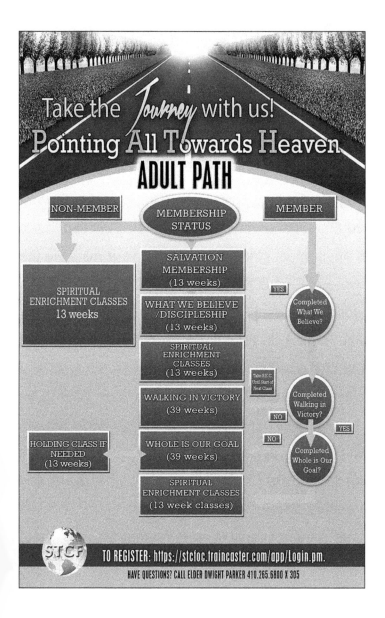

The Requirement of Stewardship

So, what is stewardship, and what does it have to do with being held accountable? Stewardship is defined as the "responsibility to manage all the resources of life for the glory of God, acknowledging God as provider" (Draper and Stewart 2003). One of the reasons that Christian basic training must start with renewing your mind via the Word of God is that stewardship is not a part of a worldly mindset. Thus, this is a trained behavior and cannot be forgotten. We are in the world but not of the world (John 17:14). God's thoughts and ways are much higher than ours (Isa. 55:8-9). In managing all our resources for the glory of God, we will be held accountable for how we as members for the body of Christ managed our time, talent, and treasury. Stewardship is not an option and requires that "paradigm shift in your thought process" that I spoke about in Chapter 1.

The worldly mindset leads us to believe that in our own ability we have achieved and rightly own everything we have. With a renewed mindset, we come to the realization that:

- The Lord is our Shepherd and provides for our needs (Ps. 23).
- The earth is the Lord's and everything in it belongs to Him (Ps. 24).
- It is God who goes before us. He is with us and will not leave us. (Deut. 31:8).
- If we remain in God, He will remain in us. Apart from God, we can do nothing (John 15:4-5).
- It is God who works in us, both to will and to work His good pleasure (Phil. 2:13).
- We can do all things through Christ because He strengthens us (Phil. 4:13).
- In Him we live, move, and have our being (Acts 17:28).

As Christians, we should be recognized by the fruit we bear (Matt. 7:16). We are no longer living to please our flesh, but we are now living for God as stated in 1 Peter 4:1–11:

"Therefore, since Christ suffered in his body, arm yourselves also with the same attitude, because whoever suffers in the body is done with sin. As a result, they do not live the rest of their earthly lives for evil human desires, but rather for the will of God. For you have spent enough time in the past doing what pagans choose to do—living in debauchery, lust, drunkenness, orgies, carousing and detestable idolatry. They are surprised that you do not join them in their reckless, wild living, and they heap abuse on you. But they will have to give account to him who is ready to judge the living and the dead. For this is the reason the gospel was preached even to those who are now dead, so that they might be judged according to human standards in regard to the body, but live according to God in regard to the spirit. The end of all things is near. Therefore be alert and of sober mind so that you may pray. Above all, love each other deeply, because love covers over a multitude of sins. Offer hospitality to one another without grumbling. Each of you should use whatever gift you have received to serve others, as faithful stewards of God's grace in its various forms. If anyone speaks, they should do so as one who speaks the very words of God. If anyone serves, they should do so with the strength God provides, so that in all things God may be praised through Jesus Christ. To him be the glory and the power for ever and ever. Amen."

Giving of our time, talent, and treasury is a God thing. Thus, we should be using our God given time, talent, and treasury to honor God and to spread the gospel. It takes a renewed mind to truly embrace stewardship. Galatians 5:17 teaches us, "The flesh desires what is contrary to the Spirit, and the Spirit what is contrary to the flesh. They are in conflict with each other, so that you are not to do whatever you want." Your sacrifice will be rewarded. God's benefits can be found throughout the Bible. From an abundant life on earth to an eternal life thereafter God's benefit package is awesome! His principle of giving states, "Whoever sows sparingly will also reap sparingly, and whoever sows generously will also reap generously. . .for God loves a cheerful giver,. . . . . Thanks be to God for His indescribable gift (2 Cor. 9:6-15)!

Whether I was serving my country in the army or serving as a member of the body of Christ, being held accountable has helped me succeed. It is a necessary part of growth and is required by God. So yes, being held accountable is a "God thing"! Our renewed minds help us to understand how important accountability truly is.

Chapter Review

1. The Bible tells us in _____
   that we will all stand before God and be held
   accountable.

2. Being _____ to the Word of God
   will change your _____ and
   your very life.

3. Hebrews 13:17 states, "_____ your
   leaders and _____to them, for they
   are keeping watch over your souls, as those
   who will have to give an _____. Let
   them do this with joy and not with groaning,
   for that would be of no advantage to you."

4. Basic training for Christians includes
   _____ and being _____
   to structured Bible study.

5. _____ is defined as the
   "responsibility to manage all the resources
   of life for the glory of God, acknowledging
   God as provider.

6. Stewardship is not an _____ and will require that "_____ _____ in your thought process" that I spoke about in chapter 1.

Application

Evaluate your current willingness to be held accountable by God?

_____

_____

_____

_____

_____

_____

What steps will you take to improve in this area?

_____

_____

_____

CHAPTER 7:

Properly Sharing the Biblical Narrative Is Essential

"Therefore go and make disciples of all nations, baptizing them in the name of the Father and of the Son and of the Holy Spirit, and teaching them to obey everything I have commanded you. And surely I am with you always, to the very end of the age." (Matthew 28:19-20)

"The Bible is the Word of God and as such should be believed and obeyed" (Elwell and Beitzel 1988, 296). As I discussed in the previous chapter, the Bible contains sixty-six books found in two sections: The Old Testament and the

New Testament. In this chapter, I will examine the Bible to explain the origin of our world (creation). I will describe how man's disobedience diverted God's original plan for mankind to live in harmony and perfect communion with Him (fall/original sin). How God redeemed the world through Jesus Christ (redemption), and how God's original plan for the world will be reestablished (restoration). This chapter will enhance your understanding of the biblical narrative and enhance your ability to share the biblical narrative with others.

Creation

In the first book of the Bible, Genesis which means beginnings, we learn that God created the heavens and the earth (1:1), the day and the night (1:5), grass and fruit trees (1:11), and every living creature in the water and on the land (1:20). God was pleased with all He made and said, "it was good" (1:25). As discussed in chapter 4, Genesis

1:26 is our first indication that God is a Triune God (the Father, the Son, and the Holy Spirit) when we read "then God said, let us make mankind in our image, in our likeness." In Genesis 1:27, God indeed creates man in His own image, both male and female. After creating mankind, God blessed them, told them to increase in number, and directed them to rule over every living creature (1:28). God gave mankind every seed-bearing plant, tree that had fruit, and all the green plants for food (1:29-30). Now, God proclaims "it was very good" (1:31)!

In Genesis 2:8, we discover that God had created a garden in Eden. "In the middle of the garden were the tree of life and the tree of the knowledge of good and evil" (Gen. 2:9). God told man that he could eat from any tree but the tree of the knowledge of good and evil because if he ate from that forbidden tree he would die (2:16-17). At this time, Adam did not have a mate, so God caused Adam to fall asleep, took one of Adam's ribs, and God made Eve (2:20-22). During this time, Adam and Eve were in harmony with God, and they could communicate with Him without hindrance.

The Fall

In Genesis 3, the serpent tricked Eve thus Adam and Eve ate from the forbidden tree. Adam disobeyed God which resulted in the **original sin**. Due to original sin now "all have sinned and **fall short** of the glory of God" (Rom. 3:23). Isaiah 59:2 tells us that sin separates us from God. Romans 6:23 tells us that, "The wages of sin is death, but the gift of God is eternal life in Christ Jesus our Lord." Now, man faces spiritual death as well as physical death. God banished Adam and Eve out of the Garden of Eden because of their sin, thus their ability to fellowship with God as intended was hindered.

In the Old Testament, we find "complex regulations by which the guilt of sin could be removed through the sacrificial system" (Manser, Dictionary of Bible Themes: The Accessible and Comprehensive

Tool for Topical Studies 2009); however, they were temporary and had to be repeated. This sacrificial system was called atonement and involved the sacrifice and offering up of the blood of a clean animal (Elwell and Beitzel 1988, 232). Isaiah 52:13 through 53:12 speaks of a future sacrifice that Jesus would make on our behalf to atone for our sins that would never have to be repeated.

Despite man's disobedience, God still loved and desired to bless His creation. "By the Abraham narrative, the author of Genesis reveals how God's promissory blessing at creation intended for all people would be acquired through Terah's son, Abram" (Matthews 2005). In Genesis 12:1-3, God told Abram to leave his country and his family to go to a land that He would reveal to him promising to make Abram a great nation. God told Abram that He would bless those who blessed him and curse those who cursed him. In Genesis 15, God came to Abram, who had no children from his wife Sarai, in a vision and promised to make his offspring as numerous as the stars in the sky. Here we see the covenant between God and Abram start to unfold. In Genesis 17, God changed Abram's name to Abraham and stated that he would be the "father of many nations," the nation of Israel, which is God's chosen people. As a sign of the covenant, God required every male in Abraham's household, both family and slaves, to be circumcised (Gen. 17:14). God also changed Sarai's name to Sarah stating that she would be the "mother of nations" (Gen. 17:15-16). God told Abraham that Sarah would have a son, and He directed Abraham to name him Isaac (Gen. 17:19).

In Genesis 22:1-13, God tested Abraham by telling him to offer his only son as a burnt offering. In obedience, Abraham prepared to offer Isaac as a sacrifice but remained faithful that God would deliver him. Rising early in the morning, Abraham, Isaac, and two young men started out on the journey to provide the sacrifice that God commanded (22:3). Upon arriving at the place God directed

Abraham to, he told the young men to stay there while he and Isaac go to worship God. Abraham, totally trusting God, told the young men that he and Isaac would return (22:5). Abraham prepared to sacrifice Isaac, but God sent a ram as a substitute (Jamieson, Fausset and Brown 1997). Through this test, Abraham showed that he trusted God and con-firmed that he would submit to God's authority. God rewarded Abraham for his obedience and again reminded him of His covenant to multiply his seed making his seed as the stars in the heaven.

By faith Abraham, when God tested him, of-fered Isaac as a sacrifice. He who had em-braced the promises was about to sacrifice his one and only son, even though God had said to him, "It is through Isaac that your off-spring will be reckoned." Abraham reasoned that God could even raise the dead, and so in a manner of speaking he did receive Isaac back from death. (Hebrews 11:17-19)

The Abrahamic covenant is still valid today. We see in Acts 3:25 that we are heirs of the covenant God made with our fathers. Other Scripture references to the Abrahamic covenant include: Romans 4:16–25; Galatians 3:6–18; 4:21–31; and James 2:21–23. The Israelites had direct access to God but wanted to be like the world, so they rejected God and asked for a king to rule over them (1 Sam. 10). Instead of maintaining their special relationship with God, the Israelites' request for a king further separated them from God.

Redemption

Reconciliation between God and humans was achieved by the birth, life, death, and resurrection of Jesus Christ (Gangel 1998, 475), which we call the gospel. The gospel can be found in the first four books of the New Testament: Matthew, Mark, Luke, and John. In Matthew 1, we see the genealogy of Jesus starts with Abraham and goes through David to our Savior Jesus Christ. Jesus "bore our sins in his body on the cross, so that we might die to sin and live for righteousness" (1 Pet. 2:24) just as was predicted in the book of Isaiah. This is an example of God's great love for us. John 3:16 tells us that "For God so loved the world that he gave his one and only Son, that whoever believes in him shall not perish but have eternal life."

In Matthew 27:50-51, we learned that after Jesus gave up his spirit the curtain of the temple that separated the Holy of Holies, which contained the ark of the covenant and the presence of God, from the Holy Place "was torn in two from top to bottom" (Matt. 27:51). The Holy of Holies was so sacred that only the high priest could enter on the Day of Atonement (Weber 2000). There is no greater love than that of Jesus Christ. He who knew no sin, loved mankind so much that He offered His blood to atone for our sins. This was the final atonement needed. Hebrews 9:15 states, "For this reason

Christ is the mediator of a new covenant, that those who are called may receive the promised eternal inheritance—now that he has died as a ransom to set them free from the sins committed under the first covenant."

The Day of Atonement

Leviticus 16 is the central passage describing and explaining the Day of Atonement ritual. Following the death of Aaron's sons Nadab and Abihu, (Lev 10), the text focuses on issues of cleanness and uncleanness of the sacred space. Chapter 16 deals with purification of the sanctuary, the high priest (16:1–4), and the people. After the high priest had achieved atonement through sacrificing a bull, he was qualified to serve in the sanctuary. The Day of Atonement ritual required two goats which were used to bring atonement for the people's sins (Cross & Livingston, 2005)

In Matthew 28, the angel announces that Jesus has risen from the dead. Before Jesus returns to heaven, He gives us clear directions in the Great

Commission. Jesus is now seated at the right hand of the Father, but He has left us the Holy Spirit (Acts 2:33). **To receive Jesus as our Savior the Bible tells us in Romans 10:9, "If you declare with your mouth, 'Jesus is Lord,' and believe in your heart that God raised him from the dead, you will be saved."** Unlike the thief (Satan) who was working through the serpent to steal, kill, and destroy mankind's destiny, Jesus has come that we may have abundant life (John 10:10). Through God's plan of salvation, we are reunited with Jesus by the indwelling of the Holy Spirit.

Restoration

Even with all we discussed above, there is still more good news! The abundant life that Jesus provides is twofold: abundant life on earth and eternal life after the return of Jesus Christ. Often, too much emphasis is placed on our eternal life with God after our death and not enough emphasis is placed on that abundant Christian life on earth in relationship with God and in community with other believers. In the words of Marva J. Dawn:

"We gather together in worship to speak our language, to read our narratives of God at work, to sing the hymns of the faith in a variety of styles, to chant and pour out our prayers until we know the truth so well that we can go out to the world around us and invite that world to share this truth with us. In our worship, we are formed by biblical narratives that tell a different story from that of the surrounding culture" (Dawn 2000).

After an abundant life on earth, God has promised us eternal life with Him. One day, in a moment, in the twinkling of an eye, our Lord and Savior Jesus Christ will come again to claim us as His own (1 Cor. 15:52). In the final book of the Bible, Revelation, which means uncovered, we learn of a new heaven and a new earth, for the first heaven and the first earth will pass away (Rev. 21:1). Christians find comfort in our knowledge that one day our relationship with God will be as it was intended to be prior to sin. Now that you have all this information, it is up to you! Do you want to be saved from your sin and receive a restored life in Jesus Christ?

Hebrews 9:27-28 states, "Just as people are destined to die once, and after that to face judgment, so Christ was sacrificed once to take away the sins of many; and he will appear a second time, not to bear sin, but to bring salvation to those who are waiting for him." If you have not made Jesus your Savior, you will not have the privilege of abundant life on earth or the blessing of eternal life in heaven. The only way to have eternal life with God is through Jesus Christ.

Conclusion

Adam's sin separated us from God, but the blood of Jesus Christ restored our access to God. Because of the completed work of salvation, mankind has been redeemed. Those who are saved will one day be reunited with God for all eternity. Believers must submit to a Spirit-filled leader who teaches and lives the Word of God, and participate to fulfill their calling. Romans 10:17 tells us that "faith comes from hearing the message, and the message is heard through the word about Christ." At church we hear the message, study the Bible, grow, fellowship, worship corporately, serve, and are held accountable. At church we learn to give of our time, talent, and treasure to help spread the gospel. As believers, we are baptized into the body of Christ (1 Cor. 12:13). We are now one with the Father, the Son, the Holy Spirit, and other members of the body of Christ.

This is just a brief summarization of the biblical story. There is a lot of powerful, life-changing information that can be found within the pages of the Bible. "For the word of God is alive and active. Sharper than any double-edged sword, it penetrates even to dividing soul and spirit, joints and marrow; it judges the thoughts and attitudes of the heart" (Heb. 4:12). To obey the Word of God and to have the ability to properly articulate the biblical narrative to others, you must continue to study to show yourself approved (2 Tim. 2:15)!

In basic training, there was great emphasis put on learning the army way. I remember how I would work so hard at making my bed quick, tight, and right—I thought. Only to have the drill sergeant to come in for inspection and tell me everything I did wrong. I would stand beside my bed in the position of attention just praying that I had gotten it right this time. Before I knew it, my mattress was flipped over, and I was on the floor doing pushups. But why did the military insist on me making my bed so tight? Training us to make our beds tight enough for a quarter to bounce was the army's way of teaching us how important it was to pay attention to details. The army wanted us to understand the importance of even the smallest detail that could save our lives. The army was trying to create a roadmap for soldiers to succeed during wartime as well as in time of peace. By flipping my bed when that quarter did not bounce on it, the drill sergeant was trying to teach, correct, and, yes, rebuke me.

Although it is important for soldiers to pay attention to details and to learn the army way, it is of greater importance for Christians to understand the biblical narrative. One of my favorite Christian writers, C.S. Lewis, could have missed his purpose because those around him were unable to teach him the biblical narrative. Born Clive Staples Lewis on November 29, 1898, in Belfast, Ireland, C.S. Lewis's giftedness was exposed at the age of four when he declared that he would only answer to the new name that he chose for himself, Jacksie (Brown

2013). Although C.S. Lewis was taken to church at an early age, his parents and teachers failed to clearly articulate the biblical narrative to him, leaving Lewis confused about God. Desperately seeking spiritual clarity, Lewis spent almost fifteen years of his adult life as an enthusiastic atheist. Thank God, Lewis finished well as one of "the most influential Christian writers of our time who continues to live on in the books he left behind" (Brown 2013, p. 2). Not only do we need to understand the biblical narrative for ourselves, we also need to be able to articulate the biblical narrative to properly disciple others. We all have an obligation according to the Great Commission to spread the gospel. This chapter was intended to help you do your part.

Chapter Review

1. The biblical narrative includes _____, _____, _____ and restoration.
2. Sin _____ us from God (Is. 59:2).

3. "The wages of sin is _____, but the gift of _____ is eternal life in Christ Jesus our Lord" (Rom. 6:23).

4. "By the _____ narrative, the author of Genesis reveals how God's promissory _____ at creation intended for all people would be acquired through Terah's son, Abram" (Matthews 2005).

5. Reconciliation between _____ and _____ was achieved by the birth, life, death, and resurrection of _____ _____ which we call the gospel.

6. Before Jesus returns to heaven, He gives us clear directions in the _____ _____.

7. The _____ _____ that Jesus provides is twofold: _____ _____ on earth and _____ _____ after the return of Jesus Christ.

Application

How will you share the biblical narrative with an unbeliever?

_____

_____

_____

_____

_____

_____

_____

_____

Epilogue

I ntentionally renewing your mind, embracing the theologian you were created to be, recognizing the power of prayer, understanding and embracing the Holy Spirit as your keeper, aggressively embracing your Christian family, willingly being held accountable, and properly articulating the biblical narrative to others are just part of your training. As Christians, we must embrace a lifestyle of learning to continually enhance our biblical worldview. During basic training, we had to learn and live by the following Soldier's Creed.

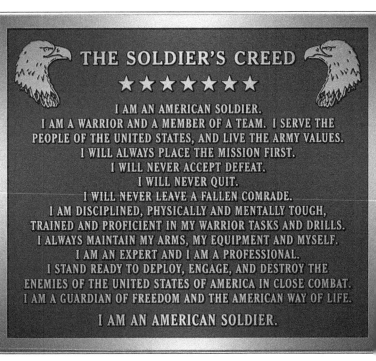

As members of the body of Christ, we need to declare our own creed.

The Christian's Creed

I am a member of the body of Christ.

I have declared with my mouth, "Jesus is Lord," and believed in my heart that God raised Him from the dead; now I am saved (Rom. 10:9).

To change my worldview, I offer my body as a living sacrifice, holy and pleasing to God, which is my true and proper worship. I am not conformed to the pattern of this world but transformed by the renewing of my mind (Rom. 12:1-2).

I declare that all Scripture is God-breathed and is useful for teaching, rebuking, correcting, and training in righteousness, equipping me for every good work (2 Tim. 3:16-17).

I am called by God, willing to humble myself, pray and seek God's face. I am committed to turning

from my wicked ways, so there will be healing in
the land (2 Chron. 7:14).

I am thankful that before Jesus ascended on high,
He gave me another advocate to help me and be
with me forever, the Spirit of truth (John 14:16-17),
which is the Holy Spirit.

I will not give up meeting together, as some are in
the habit of doing, instead, I will encourage others
as I see the day approaching (Heb. 10:25).

I will give an account of myself to God
(Rom. 14:12).

And I will continually share the Word of God,
declaring that others will not accept it as the word
of men but as the true Word of God
(1 Thess. 2:13).

To help ensure your success, Appendix A is a Spiritual Growth Chart. 1 Thessalonians 5:23 states, "And the very God of peace sanctify you wholly; and I pray God your whole spirit and soul and body be preserved blameless unto the coming of our Lord Jesus Christ" (KJV). It is God's desire that your whole spirit and soul and body be preserved blameless unto the coming of our Lord Jesus Christ. To the contrary, "the thief cometh not, but for to steal, and to kill, and to destroy: I am come that they might have life, and that they might have it more abundantly" (John 10:10). The purpose of the Spiritual Growth Chart is to help you make the paradigm shift from your original sin nature to being more like Christ. It will help you establish a holistic approach to developing an intimate relationship with Christ that is habit forming and life changing. It is God's desire that with Him at the center, we live happy, fulfilled, and healthy lives. The foundational scriptures for the Spiritual Growth Chart are Isaiah 55:8-9 and Romans 12:1-2.

Isaiah 55:8-9

"For my thoughts are not your thoughts, neither are your ways my ways, saith the LORD. For as the heavens are higher than the earth, so are my ways higher than your ways, and my thoughts than your thoughts."

Romans 12:1-2

"I beseech you therefore, brethren, by the mercies of God, that ye present your bodies a living sacrifice, holy, acceptable unto God, which is your reasonable service. And be not conformed to this world: but be ye transformed by the renewing of your mind, that ye may prove what is that good, and acceptable, and perfect, will of God."

Use the Spiritual Growth Chart to monitor the amount of time you commit to enhancing your relationship with God. These are some suggested disciplines that every Christian can benefit from.

You can add disciplines or modify the chart based on your needs. In Exodus 33:18, Moses asked God to show him His glory. This burning desire to see God's glory, to see Him face to face, is one of the most important keys to revival, reformation, and the fulfillment of God's purpose on the earth (Tenney 1998, 139). Moses simply wanted God, and that is the greatest gift and blessing we can ever give him (Tenney 1998, 140).

In addition to using the Spiritual Growth Chart, Appendix 2 contains names used to identify Jesus Christ in Scripture. Psalm 34: 1-8 states:

"I will extol the LORD at all times; his praise will always be on my lips. I will glory in the LORD; let the afflicted hear and rejoice. Glorify the LORD with me; let us exalt his name together. I sought the LORD, and he answered me; he delivered me from all my fears. Those who look to him are radiant; their faces are never covered with shame.

147

This poor man called, and the LORD heard him; he saved him out of all his troubles. The angel of the LORD encamps around those who fear him, and he delivers them. Taste and see that the LORD is good; blessed is the one who takes refuge in him."

Find a prayer partner or find yourself a quiet place to spend time with God alone. The goal is to fellowship with God. Your time with God should be delightful; enjoy it, rest in it, and celebrate it!

Colossians 1:16 states, "For in Him all things were created: things in heaven and on earth, visible and invisible, whether thrones or powers or rulers or authorities; all things have been created through Him and for Him." We were created to worship God. I pray that this book will help you enhance your relationship with God, so you will be better equipped to win the battle. You may never join the United States Army but welcome to the army of the Lord!

Bibliography

Anders, Max. *Brave new discipleship: Cultivating scripture-driven Christians in a culture-driven world.* Nashville: Thomas Nelson, 2015.

Berkhof, Louis. "The Holy Trinity." In *Systematic Theology*, by Louis Berkhof, 82-99. Grand Rapids: B. Eerdmans Publishing Co., 1938.

Boice, James Montgomery. *Psalms Volume 3.* Grand Rapids: Baker Books, 1998.

Brown, Devin. *A Life Observed: A Spiritual Biography of C.S. Lewis.* Grand Rapids: Baker Publishing Group. Kindle Edition., 2013.

Calhoun, Adele Ahlberg. *Spiritual Disciplines Handbook: Practices That Transform Us.* Illinois: InterVarsity Press. Kindle Edition, 2015.

Covey, Stephen R. *The 7 Habits of Highly Effective People: Interactive Edition.* Miami: Mango Media. Kindle Edition, 2015.

Cross, F. L., and E. A. Livingstone. "Doctrine of the Trinity." In *The Oxford Dictionary of the Christian Church*, by F. L. Cross, 1652-1653. New York: Oxford University Press, 2005.

Cross, F.L., and Elizabeth A. Livingston. *The Oxford Dictionary of the Christian Church.* New York: Oxford University Press, 2005.

Dawn, Marva J. "How Christian Worship (not Consumerist Worship) Forms a Missional Community." *The Malling of Mission: How Suburban Values Control the Church Growth Movement*, May/June 2000: Pages 28-35.

Draper, C.W., and Don H. Stewart. "Stewardship." *Holman Illustrated Bible Dictionary.* Nashville, Tennessee: Holman Bible Publishers, 2003.

Elwell, Walter A, and Barry J Beitzel. *Baker Encyclopedia of the Bible.* Grand Rapids: Baker Book House, 1988.

Erickson, Millard J. *Christian Theology.* Grand Rapids: Baker Academic, 2013.

Fort Jackson Public Affairs Office. "Fort Jackson South Carolina." *US Army Training Center and Fort Jackson.* December 3, 2016. http://jackson.armylive.dodlive.mil/ (accessed December 5, 2016).

Gangel, Kenneth O. *Holman New Testament Commentary.* Vol. 5. Nashville: Broadman & Holman Publishers, 1998.

Grenz, Stanley J, and Roger E Olson. *Who Needs Theology? An Invitation to the Study of God.* Downers Grove: InterVarsity Press, 1996.

Hendricks, Howad G., and William D Hendricks. *Living by the Book.* Chicago: Moody Press, 1991.

Humphreys, Fisher. "The revelation of the Trinity." *Perspectives In Religious Studies* 33, no. 3 (September 2006): 285-303.

Jamieson, Robert, A.R. Fausset, and David Brown. *Commentary Critical and Explanatory on the*

Whole Bible. Oak Harbor: Logos Research Systems, Inc., 1997.

Jones, G.C. "1000 Illustrations for Preaching and Teaching." 292. Nashville: Broadman & Holman Publishers, 1986.

Manser, Martin H. *Dictionary of Bible Themes: The Accessible and Comprehensive Tool for Topical Studies.* London: Martin Manser, 2009.

—. *Dictionary of Bible Themes: The Accessible and Comprehensive Tool of Topical Studies.* London: Martin Manser, 2009.

Matthews, K. A. "Genesis 11:27-50:26. Vol 1B." In *The New American Commentary*, 157-231. Nashville: Broadman & Holman Publishers, 2005.

Meeks, Charles. "Trinity." In *The Lexham Bible Dictionary*, by John D Barry, et al. Bellingham: Lexham Press, 2016.

Munroe, Myles. *Rediscovering the Kingdom.* Shippensburg: Destiny Image Publishers, Inc., 2004.

Olbricht, Thomas H. "Theologian." In *Dictionary of Christianity in America*, by Daniel G., Linder, Robert Dean Reid, Bruce L. Shelley, & Harry S. Stout. Downers Grove: InterVarsity Press, 1990.

Paul, Richard, and Linda Elder. *Miniature Guide to Critical Thinking Concepts & Tools.* Dillon Beach: Foundation for Critical Thinking, 2014.

Reinke, Tony. *Lit! A Christian Guide to Reading Books.* Wheaton: Crossway, 2011.

Sanders, Fred. *The Deep Things of God: How the Trinity Changes Everything.* Wheaton: Crossway, 2010.

Shepherd, Ernestine. *Determined, Dedicated, Disciplined To Be Fit.* Baltimore: Royal Brown Publishing, 2016.

Sire, James W. *The Universe Next Door.* Downers Grove: InterVarsity Press, USA, 2009.

Smith, James K. A. *You Are What You Love: The Spiritual Power of Habit.* Grand Rapids: Baker Publishing Group, 2016.

Soanes, C., and A. Stevenson. *Concise Oxford English Dictionary.* (11th ed.). Oxford: Oxford University Press, 2004.

Svigel, Michael J. *Retro-Christianity: Reclaiming the Forgotten Faith.* Wheaton: Crossway, 2012.

Tenney, Tommy. *The God Chasers: My Soul Follows Hard After Thee.* Shippensburg: Destiny Image Publishers, Inc., 1998.

Unknown. *Faith and Health Connection: Teaching Biblical Truths for Health and Wholeness.* 2016. http://www.faithandhealthconnection.org/the_connection/spirit-soul-and-body/ (accessed October 4, 2016).

Walker, Hezekiah. *I Need You to Survive.* 2011.

Warren, Rick. *Bible Study Methods: Twelve Ways You Can Unlock God's Word.* Grand Rapids: Zondervan Kindle Edition, 1981.

Publishers, 2000.

Williams, Thomas. *Stanford Encyclopedia of Philosophy.* Spring 2015. https://plato.stanford.edu/entries/anselm/ (accessed March 16, 2016).

.

APPENDIX A

Spiritual Growth Chart

Disciplines	Monday	Tuesday	Wednesday	Thursday	Friday	Saturday	Sunday
Prayer	30 am	30 am	30 am / 30 pm	30 am	30 am / 30 pm	30 am / 30 pm	30 am / 30 pm
Accountability Partner							
Bible Study							
Control of the Tongue							
Community							
Discipling							
Evangelism							
Fasting							
Meditation							

Prayer						
Rest						
Sabbath						
Serving						
Silence						
Solitude						
Worship						

APPENDIX B

Enhancing Your Prayer by Using Different Names of Jesus

Key Verses

Isaiah 9:6 (KJV): "For unto us a child is born, unto us a son is given: and the government shall be upon his shoulder: and his name shall be called Wonderful, Counsellor, The mighty God, The everlasting Father, The Prince of Peace."

Revelation 17:14 (KJV): "These shall make war with the Lamb, and the Lamb shall overcome them: for he is Lord of lords, and

King of kings: and they that are with him are called, and chosen, and faithful."

We can enhance our praise and worship experience by using different names of Jesus.

❖ Almighty	Revelation 1:8
❖ Alpha and Omega	Revelation 1:8
❖ Author and Finisher	Hebrews 12:2
❖ Bread of Life	John 6:35
❖ Bridegroom	Matthew 9:15
❖ Bright Morning Star	Revelation 22:16
❖ Carpenter	Mark 6:3
❖ Chief Cornerstone	Ephesians 2:20
❖ Chosen One	Isaiah 42:1
❖ Door	John 10:9
❖ Faithful and True Witness	Revelation 3:14
❖ Firstborn	Hebrews 12:23
❖ Good Shepherd	John 10:14
❖ Head of the Church	Ephesians 5:23
❖ Holy One of God	Mark 1:24
❖ Hope	1 Timothy 1:1
❖ Image of the Invisible God	Colossians 1:15
❖ Immanuel	Isaiah 7:14

❖ Last Adam	1 Corinthians 15:45
❖ Light of the World	John 8:12
❖ Man of Sorrows	Isaiah 53:3
❖ Prophet	John 6:14
❖ The Word	John 1:14
❖ Redeemer	Job 19:25

CPSIA information can be obtained
at www.ICGtesting.com
Printed in the USA
FFHW020048030519
52233625-57614FF

9 781545 6587